Contents

THE ART OF

RECRUITING VOLUNTEERS

MARK SENTER III

VICTOR BOOKS a division of SP Publications, Inc.

WHEATON. ILLINOIS 60187

Offices also in
Whitby, Ontario, Canada
Amersham-on-the-Hill, Bucks, England

Scripture quotations are from the *New American Standard Bible*,
© 1960, 1962, 1963, 1968, 1971, 1972, 1973, 1975, 1977 by the
Lockman Foundation, La Habra, California. Used by permission.

Recommended Dewey Decimal Classification: 262.15, 268.3
  Suggested Subject Heading: THE LAITY—MINISTERS OF THE CHURCH

Library of Congress Catalog Card Number: ISBN: 0-88207-297-8

VICTOR BOOKS
A division of SP Publications, Inc.
        Wheaton, Illinois 60187

Volunteers: They Can Bring Renewal (Introduction)

Volunteer lay ministry in the church began nearly 2,000 years ago during the emergence of the New Testament church in Jerusalem and Asia Minor. Even a cursory reading of Acts and the Epistles of Paul represents the early church as a closely knit body of believers, helping and serving one another in the spirit of Christ's love: "This is My commandment, that you love one another, just as I have loved you" (John 15:12). In fact, in the Apostle John's account of the Last Supper, the "love commandment" is repeated three times (John 13:34; 15:12; and 15:17) after Jesus washed His disciples' feet to illustrate the servanthood that was the heart of His ministry. The concept of service within the church, the body of Christ, is restated emphatically in James 2:17: "Even so faith, if it has no works, is dead, being by itself."

In the modern church, the concept of volunteer service has almost died under the impact of cultural fragmentation, the exaltation of individualism, and heavy economic pressures on the average American family. Ironically, the problems of fragmentation, individualism, and economic pressure are best addressed through close fellowship and strong service-oriented volunteer ministry in the church. Ministry to others, taking time to share gifts and talents, meeting others at the point of their need have a way of bringing health and wholeness to the giver as well as the one receiving the gift. Scripture tells us, "By your standard of measure, it shall be measured to you" (Matt. 7:2). All in Christ's body need to be both givers and receivers, and the church was designed originally to allow that to happen.

Lay ministry within the body of Christ is neither automatic nor spontaneous. If it were, the dynamic of service would be functioning much more freely and visibly than is happening in churches throughout the world. Rather, it must be started and sustained by "spark plugs," people who can keep the engine running. Members of the congregation must be asked to serve, assisted in identifying their gifts, then put to work in appropriate ministry.

There's a word for this process: recruitment. Properly understood and employed, recruitment is an answer to renewal in the local church.

The story is told of a Sunday School convention in which a wild rumor almost turned the place upside down. The rumor concerned an unnamed but reportedly well-known church in the heartland of the U.S., a church that *always had a surplus of volunteer workers and, consequently, a fantastic Christian education program and body life ministry.*

As the rumor went, trained teachers at this church were ready and champing at the bit to move from the "waiting list" to on-line teaching positions in new classes that continually blossomed as the educational ministry grew. Existing staff teachers seldom complained or resigned, even after 10 or more years of service, and no one at the church could remember the last time anyone quit a volunteer leadership position in midyear. The sick were visited. Needs were met in the body. Home prayer groups and neighborhood Bible studies flourished. Visitation was done by gifted volunteers, while the church grew by leaps and bounds. The pastor's Sunday messages were profoundly spiritual and deeply moving to the congregation, because he had plenty of time to pray and meditate with the Lord in developing them.

No one was quite sure where this story originated, but it spread around the convention floor like wildfire. A church without volunteer staffing problems? Pastors and Christian education directors clamored to know more about it. Was a workshop on recruitment going to be held? Where? What time? Why wasn't it listed on the convention program?

Within hours, the rumor had escaped the confines of the convention. Major publishing house representatives with curriculum display booths on the floor phoned their home companies to break the exciting news. At least two publishers assigned researchers to locate this "dream" church and to do filmstrips on its recruitment strategy. The editors of the *Wittenburg Door* pondered the news and quickly determined to give their first "Bronzed Door Award" to the rumored church (as soon as it could be found) because it so epitomized the renewal ideals the magazine advocated.

Other reactions were equally swift. Two Christian magazines assigned investigative writers to interview the pastor of this amazing church. Christian radio and television stations vied in the race to be the first to feature this "miraculous solution" to the problem of volunteer recruitment.

Then, as suddenly as the rumor began, it ended. A workshop leader from the Sunday School convention embarrassedly confessed that his workshop had been so dull that he had injected the story about the church with no recruitment problems just to wake the people up. And wake them up it did! "After all," quoted the news section of *Christianity Today*, "it gave everybody hope for their own church."

Unfortunately, hope is not built on fanciful stories to illustrate an evangelistic point, but on an honest understanding of the facts and a reasonable course of action designed in response to those facts. There are, in fact, churches with excellent recruitment programs, but for the vast majority of the churches in America, recruitment is a serious if not desperate problem. Why?

Recruitment of volunteer personnel is perhaps the most unglamorous part of the educational ministry of the local church—and yet one of the most essential. Some educators see it as the "pits." Others accept it as potential. Yet pessimist or optimist, recruitment adds up to a lot of hard work.

When I became a pastor of Christian education after 11 years of youth ministry, my greatest shock was in the area of recruitment of volunteer staff. For the first time I had to reach out beyond my immediate circle of friends to fill staff positions which had an annual turnover. A big turnover.

A slow panic set in. About 4:30 one morning I awoke with the awesome sword of staffing responsibilities hanging over my head. In those nagging hours between sleep and full consciousness, I wondered whether the pressure I

was feeling was worth the satisfaction I would experience if and when the task was accomplished. Would this kind of ministry really meet the spiritual and social needs of children, youth, and adults in the church? There was only one way to find out.

The process had begun some months earlier when, over a period of several weeks, a number of teachers had resigned for various reasons. The holes in the staff were growing and my greatest hang-up was that I had no plan or system with which to recruit volunteers for staffing ministry positions. I needed nearly 20 teachers immediately, if not sooner, and I saw no way of filling the positions.

A workshop or recruitment at a Sunday School convention provided little help. A professor from a small college gave a bone dry and hopelessly abstract picture of the art of recruitment in the local church. It seemed apparent to me that he had never felt recruitment pains similar to the ones I was experiencing. I needed practical, how-to-do-it stuff, not theory.

A phone call to a colleague-turned-professor halfway across the nation proved to be the turning point in my recruitment pilgrimage. Patiently, he explained what he had done in the three churches he had served as pastor of Christian education. A pattern began to emerge. Workable ideas began to fall into place.

The panic wasn't over. So far, I had simply outlined a few ways to channel my panic energy into a hopeful approach to solving the problem. In fact, it took over two years for me to feel really comfortable and confident with the process that eventually worked well enough to staff a Christian education program using the abilities of over 400 people in ministry to children, youth, and adults.

My uneasiness over recruitment was relieved somewhat when I began realizing that I was not alone with my burden. A trip to the West Coast a year and a half later allowed me to visit five of the best-known churches in the nation. Recruitment was a problem everywhere!

As recently as two weeks ago this same problem raised its head as I talked with one of my friends about her son, the pastor of education in a rural town church in the Midwest. "His biggest problem," said June, "is getting enough people to staff their Sunday School and youth activities."

Large church or small, professional educator or lay superintendent, rapidly growing congregation or dwindling numbers, the challenge appears to be the same: How can we recruit Christians to join in changing the lives of people within the context of the local church? This manual has been written in answer to that question. It is designed to provide a practical system of recruitment and materials which are easily adaptable for use in any congregation.

This manual is designed as a tool to assist church educators to overcome the obstacles faced in recruitment. Actually, it is a whole set of tools which can be used singly or in combination to bring real life and success to volunteer "harvesting" and thus to expanding the ministry of the local church.

Perhaps the most useful way to present these tools is to simulate a "real-life" situation in which the reader can "observe" as a new pastor of Christian education struggles with real problems to develop a successful recruiting program for his church. Though the people and events are fictional, the situations, problems, and solutions will be recognized by many as a composite drawn from the experiences of many pastors, churches, and Christian education leaders.

1

The Problem

Jeff Thompson, 26-year-old graduate of Ormsby Seminary, former star benchwarmer of Ohio State's basketball team, swung his '76 Plymouth into the staff parking lot of Walnut Heights Bible Church and pulled up next to a brand-new white Oldsmobile. The pastor's car, he assumed. Grabbing a battered briefcase, he stepped out into a brisk, chilly spring wind to get a quick look at his first church—or rather the first church to offer him the kind of job he'd prayed for: pastor of Christian education at a growing fellowship.

Nestled at the base of a hill once covered by black walnut trees, Walnut Heights Bible Church was no mean architectural feat. Jeff could tell that the complex of buildings had been designed by someone familiar with foot-traffic patterns and noise transmission problems common to larger churches, while the simple lines and soaring steeple of the church proper, communicated a simple, quiet elegance—pure white outlined against a robin's egg sky. The surrounding neighborhood was another story. Older homes, once lovely, now displayed peeling paint, overgrown hedges, cracked windows here and there, with ugly lawns still yellow-brown.

"Beauty is in the eye of the beholder," Jeff told himself as he headed for the church office, breathing a quick prayer as he walked.

Jeff was ushered into the pastor's office by Peggy, his slender blonde secretary, who put down two cups of coffee and left quietly.

Herb Wilcox stood and extended his hand. A rugged-looking man in his early 50s, the pastor could have been called handsome except for the slightly oversize nose which threw his features

out of balance. Older members of the congregation teased him about it now and then, but he took it in good humor. "Big enough to smell the will of God, small enough to keep out of other people's business," he'd say. "Besides, I need it to support my 'granny glasses.'" Somehow, the narrow steel-rimmed glasses he was referring to looked good on him.

"Good to have you on board, Jeff," Pastor Wilcox said warmly. "Is Rita happy with the house you found?"

"Yes, sir," Jeff replied, slipping out of his topcoat. "I'm sure she's going to love it here, as soon as she gets to know a few people."

"I'm glad to hear that. Let's get right down to business, Jeff. I'd like to have a word of prayer with you and a nice chat before I show you your new office."

The two men prayed brief but fervent prayers before sitting—the senior pastor behind his desk, his new assistant in one of the overstuffed chairs in front of it. Herb Wilcox lowered his head and peered at Jeff over the top of his glasses.

"Scripture says, 'Confess your sins to one another,'" the older man began. "I want us to start with a clean slate so the Lord will bless our work together. To be honest, you weren't my first choice for the job, Son—I wanted someone more experienced. But we could not afford to pay the salary of a seasoned educator. So the church board asked if I could 'live with you' as pastor of Christian education, and I said I could.

"You see, 10 years ago when I first came here, this congregation amounted to a grand total of two dozen people. It's now over 600,

9

because of the Lord's blessing, a lot of trousers with worn-out knees, and blood, sweat, and tears spent feeding and loving these sheep.

"I'm used to running the Christian Education Department out of my hip pocket," Pastor Wilcox continued, "with the help of my wife, Henrietta, and my former secretary, Alma. When Alma retired last year, Henrietta said she couldn't handle the workload herself. We had to have someone—and you're it.

"Let me level with you. My biggest apprehension is that some hotshot seminary graduate, still wet behind the ears—will be critical of my old-fashioned way of doing things and alienate my people from me. I'm concerned that he'll want to use my congregation as a guinea pig for raw, untested, speculative programs—that will hurt feelings, sow discord, and upset the progress we've made over the years. I don't want that to happen."

Jeff Thompson felt the palms of his hands beginning to sweat. Yet there was a relief at the candor of the man he would now call "pastor."

"I don't want that to happen either, Pastor Wilcox," he said quietly. "But I have to confess I've come into this job with a few apprehensions as well, and you've touched on one of them. When I was on the Ohio State basketball team, I didn't get off the bench—but I supported the first string, encouraged them, and cheered them on to win. And, they did win that year—winning the Big Ten crown. I'm a team man, Pastor, and I do my best to help the team win—whatever position I'm given. But from that experience I learned one lesson: you can't do much from the bench.

"I came here to work, to minister, to help build up the body of Christ in this church. You're the senior pastor, and I'm under your authority. You can keep me on the bench if you want to or you can put me to work where I can do some good." Jeff felt the tension rising in his voice and paused to take a deep breath and swallow.

"My greatest apprehension," the new pastor of education continued, "is that I might encounter a pastor so committed to the 'Lone Ranger' approach to church operation that he'd rather let the church go the way of the dinosaurs than allow new people and new ideas to minister life to the body.

"I've been trained in Christian education, Pastor. I've brought a lot of enthusiasm and a few ideas to this job. I believe with the Lord's leading and your advice and experience I can do well at this. I don't intend to oppose your views or experiment on the congregation. All I ask is enough freedom to serve the Lord, you, and the congregation to the best of my ability."

A smile played around Pastor Wilcox' eyes. Perhaps he understood. Maybe he could remember his idealism as he arrived at his first place of ministry. At least he was listening.

"That's fair enough, Pastor Thompson," he said. "I'm releasing you to take authority and responsibility over our Christian education program. But I would ask that every proposal for change, every new approach to problems, be brought to me for my input. As far as your relationship with the church board and Christian Education Committee is concerned, I expect you to sell your ideas to them on your own. I'll support you but I don't want to be bulldozing a path in front of you.

"Now, Jeff—I suppose you have some questions for me, so fire away."

Jeff grinned and relaxed a bit. "You 'supposed' right, Pastor, I've got hundreds of 'em."

"Well, shoot one at me and see if I can be of any help." Pastor Wilcox's sudden modesty was nearly disarming to the newcomer. This flash of insight gave Jeff a clue as to how this veteran pastor could have run the Christian education program out of his hip pocket for so many years.

"What do you think is the greatest need which Walnut Heights Bible Church faces in the educational ministry?" inquired Jeff. It was a question that he had asked a number of times during the weekend that he and Rita had candidated at the church, yet he knew that it would be an important starting place for discovering the pulse of the church from the man who knew the needs best.

"Recruitment!" was the unhesitating answer of the older man. "We've got to have more people and better prepared workers, or we are going to wear ourselves out!"

First thing the next morning, Jeff stuck his head into the walnut paneled office of his new colleague. Peggy, the pastor's secretary, had objected to the unannounced intrusion, but the self-confident newcomer assured her that he would only be with the pastor for a couple of minutes.

"Amazingly enough, Pastor, I found it! It was stashed in one of the Lay's Potato Chip boxes near the top of one of my piles."

"Good morning, Jeff," was the unenthusiastic response of the interrupted pastor.

Jeff never broke stride in his explanation. "During my internship year in Minnesota, Tim Johnson, my supervising Minister of Christian Education, had me write a paper on 'Recruitment: A Current Report.' If you would, I'd like for you to look it over and tell me if these are the same problems we are dealing with here at Walnut Heights."

Unsnapping his briefcase, he reached inside and handed Pastor Wilcox a report that looked like a seminary term paper. "I'd appreciate it if you'd let me know what you think."

As abruptly as he had entered, Jeff retraced his steps to the outer office, 106 seconds had elapsed. Pastor Wilcox thumbed through the report and began to read.

RECRUITMENT

For the purpose of this project, "recruitment" means the obtaining of suitable Christian leaders from the congregation who will meet children, youth, and adults at the point of their need and guide them into a growing maturity in Christ through the educational agencies of the local church.

There are several words which stand out as key in this definition and deserve greater amplification. "Obtaining" does not mean coercion, manipulation, or a life sentence at "hard labor" in the Beginner Department. "Obtaining" simply means plugging people who want to serve God into sockets of spiritual need. It is the natural way of drawing the spiritual current from one person and passing it along to another, less mature person. Sometimes this involves a need which can be met. At other times it means assisting a person in discovering latent spiritual gifts and natural talents. Usually "obtaining" means asking a Christian to accept a specific responsibility for a designated amount of time.

"Suitable Christian leaders" is a phrase which recognizes that not everyone is cut out to assist wiggly three-year-olds or obnoxious junior high students in discovering God's truths in the Bible. In fact, more people are not suited for any specific ministry position than are uniquely suited. Some are not really Christians; others cannot lead; and still others find themselves mismatched due to temperament, training, background, or any one of a number of God-given factors. But the exciting part of recruitment of "suitable Christian leaders" is that God does not allow a ministry need to develop without providing a person to meet that need.

The "point of their need" takes into account that people are unique. Each person develops at his own rate and in response to various circumstances. Physical limitations, emotional stress, and family upheaval as well as the normal transitions of life rub the "point of need" raw—making the person receptive to the healing oil of a Christian's ministry. Everyone has a need to be loved by a godly adult and to be taught eternal truths appropriate for his age-level, and this is most effectively done in relationship to personal needs.

"Growing maturity in Christ" is a phrase adapted from Colossians 1:28: "We proclaim Him [Christ], admonishing every man and teaching every man with all wisdom, that we may present every man complete [mature] in Christ." The maturing process will only be complete when a person stands before God as an individual whose name is written in the Book of Life (Rev. 20:15). Until then, however, the maturing process continues and the church is God's practice field in which this maturing takes place. Other believers, then, are the instructors and coaches for this maturing process.

The "educational agencies of the local church" will differ from church to church. In renewal oriented congregations, the "agencies" may be revised each year or two, but leadership is still needed even though the process of recruiting may take a more passive form. For most churches, however, Sunday School, children's church, choirs, club programs, and youth groups will constitute the primary agencies for which Christian leaders are needed.

OBSTACLES

Meanwhile, facing reality, we find that recruitment may always be a problem. It sounds so easy when definitions are laid out and theological jargon is spun into neat webs of logic. But when it comes to obtaining a chairman for the club committee, certain factors make the process difficult. Therefore, before we look at the process of recruitment, we would be wise to look at the obstacles which impact the local church in its recruitment of volunteer ministers.

Always a Problem—Lest we become too discouraged with the apathy which is found in our society, let's remind ourselves that recruitment of volunteers has always been a problem. Ezekiel records the Lord as saying, "I searched for a man among them who should build up the wall and stand in the gap before Me for the land that I should not have to destroy it, but I found no one" (Ezek. 22:30). The Lord Jesus in commissioning 72 of His followers to go out in ministry, reminded them that "the harvest is plentiful, but the laborers are few" (Luke 10:2). The history of the Sunday School movement portrays a constant picture of inadequately staffed mission fields. A review of the minutes of the Christian Education Committee from years gone by or a conversation with former Sunday School superintendents will quickly reveal that the recruitment problem is not a new phenomenon. Yet it has been further complicated by cultural obstacles as we approach the end of the 20th century.

Movement Away from Volunteerism—Our society seems to be moving away from the very idea of volunteerism. Perhaps the best example of this is the United States military. During World War II and the Korean conflict there was a draft, yet men "willingly" volunteered to serve in the armed forces. With the advent of the unpopular Vietnam conflict, young men and women ceased to feel the moral imperative to serve. "Never volunteer for anything," is advice often heard in all of the armed services.

The church, caught up in the "pay-me-what-I'm-worth" cultural mentality, is finding itself more and more dependent on paid staff members and less and less on the volunteers who at one time were the backbone of the church's ministry. Though many of these paid staff members have become facilitators for assisting volunteers to serve more effectively, many paid professional staff have become nothing more than replacements for volunteer ministers.

Working Women—More than half of the women in the United States are working at jobs outside the home. Many of these women are married and share the responsibility for the family with their husbands. However, much of the volunteer "manpower" of days gone by was provided by women—housewives, primarily. Women had more discretionary time and therefore could spend more time in service to the church or to the community. Women assumed most of the responsibility for the care of the home, often supervising the children in performing some of the household chores. This freed the men to serve part-time in volunteer capacities in the church. Now, with the high-pressured demands of society and economy, families have less discretionary time and therefore guard it more jealously, leaving many of the responsibilities at the church untended.

Absentee Fathers—At the same time that mothers have been working more, fathers have been putting in longer and longer hours in order to achieve the elusive dream perpetuated by the success syndrome of our culture. The suburban sprawl of homes surrounding the major cities of the nation have made commuting a way of life. In many families the father spends two to three hours each day traveling to and from his job. When added to an eight- or nine-hour workday and the possibility of a second job during the evening to make ends meet, the church has lost another potential volunteer who is hardly able to give his family enough quality time to keep it together, much less provide any kind of volunteer help with projects or ministry responsibilities at the church.

Success of Adult Classes—While these factors have been taking place outside church, there has been a change in the philosophy of Christian education within the local church. The baby boom of the '40s has grown up to be the dominant generation within the church. With this has come an emphasis on adult continuing education. Adult Sunday School classes have taken on a very important role in the church, not only for teaching biblical truth but also for providing the basis for social relationships and spiritual intimacy. The midweek service has declined in importance because of hectic schedules of members of the congregation. Sunday School classes, on the other hand, have increased in importance, for much of the spiritual support and encouragement which was previously received at a midweek service is now being received in adult Sunday School classes. Consequently, adults tend to be less likely to volunteer for service opportunities in the church at a time which would take them away from their own Sunday School classes.

Social Isolation of Teachers—in contrast to the rising social importance of the Sunday School class is the tendency of teaching responsibilities to isolate children's Sunday School teachers from fellowship with the church family. In much the same way that mothers at home encounter frustration over seldom being able to carry on conversations with friends and other adults, teachers may lose contact with their peer groups. As a result, a teacher may choose to teach a class for only one year and then return to his or her adult class in order to reestablish some of the friendships which have been "sacrificed" during the year.

"Me" Orientation—One of the legacies left to the church by the Vietnam War generation and its concurrent protest movement is the phrase, "I've Gotta Be Me!" popularized by the musical *Hair*. The narcissism of the protest movement and growing drug culture of the '60s has now influenced our culture to become an accepted part of life. Activities in the church have been significantly devalued. The pleasure or satisfaction of the individual has become the standard by which every activity is measured. Thus, if a need for volunteers in the Christian education program is announced, a typical response of the "me" generation, as author Tom Wolfe called it, is "What will I get out of it? What will I have to give up?" rather than "How can we as a church get this task accomplished?"

Lack of Theology of Service—In our consumer-oriented society the value of an activity is most frequently judged by the benefit derived from it. Much of the time a sense of gratification is derived from receiving the most benefit with the least effort. This worldly attitude has invaded the church to the extent that the value of one's quiet time may be judged on the amount of "blessing" one has gotten out of his devotions. Christ's example of washing His disciples' feet and the lesson of servanthood it embodies seem to have been forgotten.

The "gimme" mind-set has carried over into volunteer ministry in the church. It is often the case that a parent will choose not to teach Sunday School until his or her child is old enough to be in the Sunday School program. In order to make sure that the child receives a good Sunday School education, the parent will make a commitment. But the commitment is not to service. It is a commitment to protect one's own interests.

Project Orientation—Long-term commitments may be a thing of the past. Today, people tend to be project oriented. There is a great desire to be able to get into a job, get it done, and go on to the next thing.

The YMCA has discovered in its use of volunteers that many people prefer to volunteer 50 hours of service over a four-week period of time rather than spread it over six months or a year. We've developed a sort of immersion psychology. A businessman is more likely to be willing to sell Christmas trees for the YMCA between Thanksgiving and Christmas, spending four hours a night and five hours on Saturdays to fulfill his responsibility, than to teach a skill to senior citizens once a week. The latter apparently ties up too much time and limits other "project type" commitments that the volunteer might want to make.

The impact of this mind-set on the educational program of the church is that a person would generally rather volunteer as a day camp worker or teacher in Vacation Bible School (and exhaust himself/herself in one week of ministry) rather than make a year-round commitment to teach in the Sunday School program.

Fears—There are many fears associated with taking a volunteer ministry position in a local church. One such fear is the "I'll-never-get-out-of-it" phobia. It is based on the myth of the faithful lady in the Beginner Department who has been teaching for the past 20 years without so much as a year's sabbatical leave. There is no way that the average young adult wants to get locked into a situation like that.

A second fear is the "what-if-the-kids-go-wild?" phobia. Of all the people I have interviewed for teaching positions in childrens' educational programs, this is the most commonly expressed apprehension. Parents may have difficulty in handling their own children, and they wonder how in the world they will be able to control, not 1 or 2, but 8 or 10 children in a confined classroom area.

The "what-if-they-know-more-than-I-do?" phobia is a third major fear. This is felt many times by the new Christian who is aware of the possibility that children (especially older ones) who attend a Christian day school and thus have been exposed to teaching from the Bible on a daily basis, might be attending the class. It is the possibility of being embarrassed before all the children of the class which sometimes causes discomfort within the potential teacher. Similar fears keep some gifted adults from volunteering to teach adult Sunday School classes.

It Is Someone Else's Job—One of the greatest obstacles to recruitment in the local church is that the responsibility is so freely passed along to other people. The senior pastor expects the pastor of Christian education to do it. The pastor of Christian education expects the recruitment committee to do it. The recruitment committee expects the department superintendents to do it. The department superintendent expects the Sunday School cabinet to do it. The Sunday School cabinet expects the Christian education pastor to do it. The buck is passed from person to person and from group to group. There is very little "ownership" of the responsibility and, therefore, the task too often falls on the already overloaded shoulders of one or two key people.

Vacuum of Prayer—The Lord Jesus told His disciples to pray that the Lord of the harvest would thrust forth workers into His harvest fields. The same need is evident today—the people of the local church need to be in prayer that God would thrust forth workers into their harvest fields through the teaching and evangelistic programs of the church. Yet those prayer meetings tend to become more like the hospital auxiliary or unemployment bureau or even a counseling center where troubled individuals and marriages are prayed for. The importance of these areas is undeniable, yet prayer for them must not rule out fervent intercession for church needs and programs that minister health to the entire body.

In "The Marva Collins Story," the television version of a preparatory school's efforts to provide quality education to disadvantaged black children on the West Side of Chicago, Marva asked a discouraged youngster, "How do you eat an elephant?"

"One bite at a time!" was the child's timid response.

One bite at a time can turn an obnoxious responsibility into a palatable, if not tasty, feast.

* * *

Wednesday, Pastor Wilcox invited Jeff to lunch at a local restaurant. Over hot roastbeef sandwiches, the senior pastor casually remarked, "That report of yours on recruitment—very interesting stuff."

2

Who Does the Recruiting?

Jeff Thompson, the lanky new pastor of Christian education at Walnut Heights Bible Church, squirmed uncomfortably in his chair in the waiting room, pushed his glasses back on his nose with a nervous gesture, and shuffled once again through the sheaf of papers in his manila folder. Two months had flown by since Jeff had joined the "real world" of church ministry. The soft rhythmic clatter of the secretary's electric typewriter punctuated the morning with that "getting-things-done" atmosphere that Pastor Herb Wilcox demanded of all paid staff.

Abruptly, the door to the pastor's office pushed open, and Pastor Wilcox's head poked out, gray eyes twinkling over his granny glasses. "Come in, Jeff," he said. "Let's have a look at what you've worked up. And, Peggy, bring us some coffee, please—and hold all calls during our conference time—excepting my wife, of course."

"Yes, Pastor Wilcox." Like Jeff, the pretty blonde secretary was a relative newcomer and hadn't yet earned the privilege of using the more familiar "Pastor Herb" form of address.

Jeff settled in the overstuffed chair in front of the pastor's desk, smiling his thanks as Peggy handed him a steaming cup of coffee. Pastor Wilcox flipped open Jeff's manila folder, sipped his coffee, and tossed an absent minded "thank you" after his departing secretary. Running a hand through his still thick, wavy, gray-blond hair, the older man mused over the top page, lost in thought. "We've run our education program by personal touch for so long, I can hardly believe there is any other way of doing it."

"There may not be," affirmed Jeff.

Pastor Wilcox cleared his throat and began to read from the paper in front of him. "Educational staff—39 Sunday School teachers, 18 children's church leaders, 20 children's club leaders, 8 youth group sponsors, 8 home Bible study leaders, and 7 committee members and officers. Total—100 volunteer staff members." The pastor let out a low whistle. "Is that all?"

"No, sir. That doesn't include the nursery workers. They're on a separate list—volunteers rotate from month to month."

"You've really done your homework, Son," Pastor Wilcox commented. "Is this a list of current volunteers?"

"Not exactly," Jeff explained. "We'll be losing about a dozen by next fall—four of the ladies are pregnant, six families are moving out of town, and two of the men will be working Sundays. And, I'd like to recruit eight more to reduce class sizes."

"So, you'll need to recruit about 20 new volunteers." Pastor Wilcox picked up his pen and began to scrawl a note. "I'll just tell Henrietta we need to 'lean a little' on a few old-timers. We'll get your 20 recruits, Son."

"Please, sir," Jeff offered. "Let me try it my way. I'll have to break in sometime, and it might as well be now."

Pastor Wilcox's eyebrows lifted a notch. "Do you know what you're getting into, Jeff? It's going to take you 10 phone calls to find 1 volunteer. And, because you're new, the people you phone are going to toss questions at you for half an hour before letting you go. That's five hours of phone calls to get a single volunteer, and even then your recruit may be a washout when you speak face to face with the person.

We're looking at a solid month's work to fill 20 volunteer positions."

"Maybe six weeks," Jeff admitted. "I agree, that's a lot of work—especially when I'm planning on organizing a father-and-son canoe trip, participating in summer youth camp, and taking a week of vacation with my wife, Rita. If I had to do it all myself, it might never get done—at least not right, anyway."

The senior pastor peered at him over his glasses. "I suppose you have a trick up your sleeve?"

"In a way." Jeff laughed. "I just believe recruitment is everybody's responsibility. I plan on asking for help."

Pastor Wilcox reddened. "I just offered help—and you refused. I really don't understand this at all!"

"No offense intended, Pastor," Jeff said gently. "I realize I was hired to take the recruitment problem off your shoulders, and that ironically I need your help at the same time—as well as assistance from other leaders in the church. But I wanted to know what the Bible had to say about recruiting—so I went back to the drawing board, so to speak.

"It's all in that folder right on your desk." Jeff pointed. "Take your time, Pastor Wilcox. I plan to give copies to members of the Christian Education Committee, and the adult Sunday School teachers, too."

Puzzled but curious, the senior pastor turned back to the report on his desk as his young "wet-behind-the-ears" seminary graduate assistant slipped quietly from the room. He began to read the report.

★   ★   ★

Recruitment and the Holy Spirit

Though the task of recruiting workers for the educational program may seem overwhelming and at times awesome, the responsibility does not lie with pastors of Christian education alone. The One ultimately in charge of providing workers is the Spirit of God. In fact, three of His major activities in the life of a believer are related to voluntary Christian service:

1. *Filled to Serve*—Following Christ's resurrection, the disciples were told to remain at Jerusalem until they received the Holy Spirit who would empower them to serve as bold witnesses for the kingdom of God (Acts 1:4-8). Later, as Paul writes to the Ephesian church, he reminds them that they are to be filled with the Holy Spirit. This filling will in turn produce a willingness to submit to or serve one another (Ephesians 5:18-19, 21).

Perhaps this is why new Christians frequently volunteer to accept teaching positions or work in club programs. The realization of what Christ has done in their lives has so filled them with a sense of joy and responsibility that they are eager to share this news with other people.

2. *Gifted to Serve*—Earlier in this same letter, the Apostle Paul speaks of spiritual gifts that have been given to the church. These gifts have come in the form of uniquely equipped individuals who are able to prepare God's people for their responsibility of building up and strengthening the Christian community (Ephesians 4:11-13). Though the variety of gifts is better described in 1 Corinthians: 12—14, the same emphasis holds true in Paul's letter to the Corinthians: gifts are for edifying or building up the body of Christ.

A strange mind-set has infected the church in recent years related to the use of spiritual gifts. Instead of accepting gifts as a means to serve other Christians, many people in the local church have assumed a showcase mentality, placing their spiritual gifts on display for other people to see, but they are not touched by them. There is much more talk about spiritual gifts in some churches than there is of using them for serving the body of Christ.

The object of spiritual gifts, to build up the body of Christ, was evident in the early church as it was built up in both numbers (quantity) and in spiritual maturity (quality). Today, the Holy Spirit is just as anxious to produce these same results in the local church through the ministries of Spirit-filled and gifted people.

3. *Fruit to Serve*—A third major function of the Holy Spirit is that of producing fruit. The fruit of the Spirit, listed in Galatians 5:22-23, is love, joy, peace, patience, kindness, goodness, faithfulness, gentleness, and self-control. The description of these qualities of Christian living as "fruit" is most fitting. A tree does not bear fruit so it can proudly proclaim that it has grown apples or pears on its branch. Instead,

bearing fruit is a process natural to a healthy tree. The fruit is enjoyed, not by the tree itself, but by someone else who has picked the fruit to eat it, to be nourished and strengthened by it.

Fruit is enjoyed most when it comes as a gift. Somehow, our society has reversed that concept. Besides making the possession of the gift more important than the use of the gift, some Christians are writing books about the various fruit of the Spirit as if to proclaim the intrinsic value of the fruit itself. It seems to have been forgotten that the fruit has to be shared, consumed to fulfill its purpose.

The entire context of the passage about the fruit of the Spirit is that of Christian service. "For you" states the Apostle Paul, "were called to freedom, brethren; only do not turn your freedom into an opportunity for the flesh, but through love serve one another" (Gal. 5:13).

The Holy Spirit will be doing His job of recruiting long before the summer recruitment drive begins. The Holy Spirit has always filled certain believers for service; He has gifted them in ways to delight the perceptive pastor or superintendent. At the same time, He has given people within the congregation fruit which they need to give away. These assurances should encourage leaders involved in recruiting volunteers in the local church.

Pastor—Creates Consciousness

In most churches it is the pastor's responsibility to promote a climate in which Christian service is an essential element of Christian living. In some churches, depending on the size, personality, and personal preferences of the pastor, the senior minister may find himself deeply involved in the recruitment process or occasionally active in the ongoing task. But no matter what the size of the church, the pastor has a vital role in the recruitment process as he preaches and teaches from God's Word. In many ways, the teachers of the adult classes within the church share this same responsibility.

There are five primary ways in which the pastor can establish a climate of service through his teaching and preaching ministry:

1. *Teach Service*—Scripture is filled with the mandate to obey God and serve mankind in both the spiritual and physical realms. From Genesis 2, where God places Adam in the Garden of Eden to "work it and take care of it" to the Book of Revelation where the churches are told by the messenger from God to repent, the concept of physical and spiritual service dominates Scripture. Thus it becomes the pastor's responsibility, in proclaiming the whole counsel of God, to teach the importance, not only of hearing the Word but of "doing it" as well.

2. *Model Service*—Though it is difficult for the senior pastor to be deeply involved in the educational program, there are many ways in which he can model Christian education before his congregation. A pastor may discuss variety in approaches that teachers may take to a given lesson. He may volunteer to give a devotional, lead a game time, or explain a hobby in the club program of the church at least once or twice a year. Camp, Vacation Bible School, or some aspect of the music program may provide an opportunity for him to model his commitment to Christian service above and beyond his primary commitment of preaching. The more people see "live" examples of Christian service and not just hear verbal teaching, the more they will be willing to follow this example.

One note of caution. "Modeling" does not mean taking over the responsibility. The ownership and thus the responsibility for the various educational ministries could easily slip onto the shoulders of a pastor merely attempting to model what he was teaching. This would only serve to frustrate both the pastor and ultimately the educational staff.

3. *Illustrate Service*—A senior pastor once commented, "The last person to speak to me before I go on the platform is likely to get quoted." It was not that he would go to the pulpit unprepared, for he was extremely articulate and spoke without notes. He was, however, wise enough to make use of fresh illustrations even if he had not previously planned to do so. Therefore, from time to time, the Christian education pastor would feed him appropriate information just before a given service so that he, in turn, could share the joy of the educational ministry through current illustrations of what God had been doing.

This desire to know and to share what has been happening should be widely understood throughout the church. In many churches the only reason volunteer group leaders phone the pastor is to discuss or report something negative. People in educational ministries should share the positive experiences of their ministry with their pastors—testimonies about what God has been doing in their departments. Pastors can then find ways to share this, whether from the pulpit, in small group discussions, or with the church board. Any way it is done, the affirmation and encouragement which come as a result of successful accounts of ministry will make the process of recruitment easier throughout the church.

4. *Feature Service*—A pastor who is a vital part of the recruitment process will frequently provide opportunities for people to testify as to what has been happening in their areas of ministry. Testimonies can be a vital part of the congregational life as people share the joys and sometimes the agonies of ministering within a fellowship. The Christian Education Committee and board members need to be exposed to the life-changing events which happen as a result of the policies and financial support which they have provided. Congregational business meetings can be turned into times of celebration as the harvest from a year of labor is surveyed and then dedicated to the Lord.

5. *Stimulate Service*—In most churches the pastor is the person who is most attuned to the spiritual gifts which have been granted to the church. He can watch the gifts bud, bloom, and mature in the lives of his parishioners. As he sees these gifts as well as the fruit of the Spirit mature, he can use his influence to stretch an individual in growing. It is much like a high school football coach who sees potential in the spindly form of a freshman quarterback; the trained eye of the coach sees confidence, ability to throw accurately, a quick sure hand, and agility amid the rush of opposing linemen. The coach will then refine this raw talent and work to bring it to maturity. Similarly, the pastor, because of his trained sensitivities, has the opportunity to single out and develop leadership from within his congregation in order to recruit the best people for service within the local church.

Pastor of Christian Education— Guides the Gifted

The pastor of Christian education has the potentially most rewarding position within the church staff. It is his opportunity to work with the people within the congregation in order to discover their spiritual gifts and ministry preferences. Then he has the privilege of providing places of service to these people whom God has prepared for ministry. In order for the CE pastor to accomplish this task, six distinct functions must be handled in either a formal or informal manner:

1. *Understand People-Needs*—Before the pastor of Christian education can begin recruiting and placing workers, he must understand the needs of his congregation and which of those can be met through the Christian education ministry. A distinction needs to be made at this point. When we speak of needs, we are not referring to positions which need to be filled (though that must be kept clearly in mind). Instead we are talking of the "people-needs" which are crying out for help, support, and teaching.

People-needs may refer to a particular child who needs special loving care. People-needs may refer to the sparks that are ignited when a certain class of junior high boys come together. People-needs may refer to the basics of our faith which a new believer desires to learn and understand. People-needs may refer to a challenge from a loving adult which will result in a vibrant Christian witness on the campus of the local community college. Whatever these people-needs are, the pastor of Christian education has the responsibility to know them before he can effectively recruit people to meet those needs.

2. *Discover Gifts of Believers*—A person with a knowledge of people-needs and no knowledge of how to meet those needs will be frustrated. Most ministers have experienced this at one time or other because their sensitivity to needs far exceeds the recognition of spiritual gifts within the congregation. Thus it becomes the responsibility of the pastor of Christian education, and in some cases the superintendent of the Sunday School, to be constantly watching for the manifestation of gifts, even in embryonic fashion, among his parishioners.

The recognition of gifts also implies personal conversations *with* people, discussing their inclinations for service, and *about* people, discussing the emerging manifestations of gifts which may have not been discovered by the

Christians who possess them.

Perceptive pastors and Christian leaders find that the Holy Spirit provides gifted people to meet every spiritual need which He desires to have met at a given time. The problem of recruitment comes, not because of a lack of appropriate people, but because we have not activated the resources which God has provided in the local church.

3. *Connect Gifts with Needs*—This is not a rush process. Nor is the task accomplished in one short recruitment push in late summer or early fall. The introduction process is as delicate as that of introducing your daughter to your best friend's nephew who has just returned from his second year in college. You want to create the opportunity for a relationship to develop without pushing so hard as to destroy the possibility.

It's almost as if the pastor of Christian education is merely a spokesman for God, a provider of information, and a resource for people who desire spiritual development.

4. *Interview Volunteers*—It is very important for the pastor of Christian education to interview volunteers before placing them in ministry positions for two primary reasons. First, the pastor of Christian education needs to have as thorough a knowledge of his volunteer staff as possible in order to wisely place each person in need-meeting positions. Second, the pastor of Christian education needs to understand the expectations and fears of the volunteer in order to assure him that his expectations will be met and that support will be available to handle those aspects of the ministry which generate apprehension.

5. *Assign Workers*—When the needs of individuals in the congregation and the gifts of the volunteer are clearly understood, no one in the congregation is better equipped to assign the person to a job than the pastor of Christian education. He may choose to solicit the assistance of a church committee to broaden his insights, but since he is functioning as the executive director of the Christian education program he is ultimately responsible for the placement and (if necessary) the removal of volunteers in ministry. Any system which removes the responsibility of placement from the pastor of Christian education is either compensating for deficiencies in that pastor or

tying his hands. Neither should ever occur.

6. *Cultivate Continued Gift Development*—Once a person has been placed in a ministry, that does not end the relationship between the pastor of Christian education and that volunteer. In fact, in some ways the relationship needs to grow stronger as the pastor of Christian education continues to assist his co-worker in developing and perfecting his gifts and ministry preferences. A note of encouragement after a firsthand classroom observation, an article on an area of interest relating to one's spiritual gifts, the suggestion of a workshop to attend or resource person to be sought out, are all ways which can contribute to the development of a Christian education worker.

The implications of the Christian education pastor's responsibilities are twofold. First, he needs to be out among the people discovering needs and gifts, asking questions, making observations, listening, supporting. The pastor of Christian education who expects to work from his office and dictate orders, write creative bulletin announcements, and develop programs on paper will rarely succeed in recruitment.

Second, the pastor of Christian education should remain in the same church for several years, at least. No matter how hard he works, he will never be able to discover the needs of the people in one or two years. Gift potential is similarly hard to detect on a one-shot basis. Insights are gathered slowly and pieced together as a person matures, not only in his spiritual life but also in his physical and mental capacities. Putting all of this together, the pastor of Christian education who succeeds in recruitment will become most effective when he has spent a number of years discovering needs, identifying gifts, and introducing the people who possess them.

Christian Education Committee— Monitors the Ministry

The Christian Education Committee need not be actively involved in the recruitment process except on an informal or task-related basis. As individuals, the committee members will probably want to participate in the recruitment process, but they are not the ones who are primarily responsible for the task.

In fact, if the Christian Education Committee members become active in the recruitment process it can become a negative reward system. By this I mean a person can be asked to do one job (serve on the Christian Education Committee) and when he does a good job as a committee member he is "rewarded" with a second job, that of recruiting new volunteer staff members. This negative reward system frequently assures that neither one of the jobs will be done well and that frustrations may set in as the committee members feel overwhelmed by the responsibilities placed on them.

There are, however, specific responsibilities which the Christian Education Committee can and should shoulder as a group and as individuals:

1. *Monitor Needs and Personnel*—One of the responsibilities of the Christian Education Committee is to know what is happening in the education program. Because the volunteer staff members are so vital to the ministry process, it is important that the committee members know the concerns and joys of the ministry.

Prayer should be a vital ministry of the Christian Education Committee. As they pray for needs to be met through people they should also assure their volunteer staff that specific prayer requests are being remembered each time the committee meets.

2. *Continually Look for Gifted People*—The Christian Education Committee is the eyes and the ears of a pastor of Christian education. Just as he is looking for gifted people and unmet needs, the committee should be doing the same thing. The use of specific gifts should be encouraged by committee members; ideas of which person should be sought to meet a specific need should be passed along to be acted on by the pastor of Christian education through the channels he has set up.

3. *Individually Plant Seed Thoughts*—A person does not cease to be a committee member once he leaves a committee meeting. His function merely changes. Instead of making policy he becomes an advocate for Christian education. One of the best ways to do this is by planting seed thoughts in the minds of people who attend the church.

A seed thought is an idea or suggestion made at an appropriate time in a loving manner. "Have you ever thought of teaching?"/"You're really gifted with adults."/"What do you think your ministry is going to be during the coming year?"/"You are really skilled with your hands. Have you ever thought of working in our Media/Resource Center?" These and many other comments might be dropped into a normal conversation and lay the groundwork for someone to approach that same person at a later date with a specific ministry in mind.

4. *Approve Financial Resources*—Recruitment is usually made much easier when the recruiter can assure a volunteer that the church has provided resources to assist in equipping new teachers and leaders through training workshops and seminars.

Adequate equipment and supplies either purchased by the church or reimbursed from the Christian education budget let a new teacher know that he is considered important by the leadership of the church. The Christian education budget should make room for curricular material and also for equipment, supplies, awards, supplementary materials, honorariums for outside resource people, and a multitude of variations within these categories.

5. *Affirm Existing Staff*—Two primary factors will encourage a teacher to continue with his teaching responsibility—achievement and affirmation. Achievement means that a person feels as if he is doing a good job. This feeling may be based on the fact that he has done everything that is in his job description as a teacher of fourth-grade boys during a given year. It may be based on the fact that one or more of his students have made a profession of faith during the time he was their teacher. It may be based on the nonverbal cues given by students in class.

The second important factor is that of affirmation. People need to be patted on the back while doing the Lord's work. Some churches provide a recognition dinner at the end of the year to which all of the teaching staff are invited free of charge. Other Sunday Schools recognize certain individuals as teacher, superintendent, or club leader of the year as a way of affirming outstanding work.

By whatever means it is done, the Christian Education Committee should be among the most aggressive "affirmers" in the church.

Department Leaders and Teachers—
Sharing the Satisfaction

To avoid the negative reward system, as in the case of the Christian Education Committee, the teaching staff should not be made primarily responsible for recruitment within the Christian education program. However, there is nothing quite so compelling as the person who is excited about his ministry opportunities and wants others to share in the joy of ministry. Thus the department leaders and teachers have the following responsibilities:

1. *Share the Satisfactions of Teaching*—The more people in the church hear about the joys of ministry both from the pulpit and from the teaching staff, the easier it will be to find volunteers to be part of this ongoing ministry. Though it may sound crass, everybody loves a winner—person, ministry, or program. As a teaching staff talks about the lives that have been touched through the educational ministry of the church, people will want to become part of that ministry.

2. *Direct People to the Pastor of Christian Education*—There is a tendency for the sincerely interested volunteer to become a recruitment and placement committee all combined in one. Despite any advantages there may be in capitalizing on a person's enthusiasm to recruit others to work with them, the pastor of Christian education needs to retain the responsibility and control of placement. It is quite possible that as he interviews a person recently recruited by an excited teacher, he will discover this person's talents might be better used somewhere else in the church. The insight that the CE pastor can provide may insure a longer and more meaningful period of service to the body of Christ.

It is the responsibility of each teacher to direct new recruits to the pastor of Christian education who will, in turn, place that person in a ministry situation which will maximize the use of his spiritual gifts.

3. *Work to Make the Teaching Team Effective*—If each Sunday School teacher is working only for himself and is not attempting to be part of the teaching team to which he has been assigned, isolation will occur. The only factor which would keep the teaching team together would be their common concern for the children they teach. Consequently, there

would come a drifting apart and a lack of mutual support and encouragement.

By contrast, the teaching team members who work together and support one another find that there is little turnover in their departments. Consequently, there is no need to recruit new workers as often for those departments. Also, a loving family atmosphere is created which becomes attractive to new or potential teachers.

Personnel Committee—
Contacts the Congregation

A Personnel Committee may be formed either as an ad hoc committee which serves for a limited period of time in order to survey the congregation or as a standing committee which is constantly assisting the pastor of Christian education in the recruitment process. The committee should be composed of people who are gifted in interpersonal relationships and are willing to take the time to talk with people—on the phone, face to face, in informal settings, or by personal appointment.

The responsibilities of the Personnel Committee, however, are fairly straightforward. They include the following:

1. *Survey Every Active Member of the Church*—For the most part this will mean making phone calls to the adults in the church on a systematic basis. The object of these phone calls is merely to discover what area of ministry a person foresees for himself in the coming year.

Contrary to what might be imagined, most people greatly appreciate a phone call and are willing to talk about the needs of the church and their own areas of interest.

2. *Explain Needs to Interested People*—If a person is to effectively explain the needs of the education program, the pastor of Christian education or the Sunday School superintendent will need to provide that information to Personnel Committee members. With that in hand, the Personnel Committee members can be on the lookout for specific types of people who can meet specific types of needs.

3. *Direct Pastor of Christian Education to Contact Interested People*—Once the interest has been discovered, that information needs to be passed along to the pastor of Christian education as quickly as possible so that appro-

priate interviews may be set up prior to the waning of the initial interest. Thus the committee members need to touch base with the pastor of Christian education at least once a week and, at times, more frequently than that.

Membership Committee— Challenges the Committed

As people join the church there is a tendency to merely put their names on the church roll; they then do nothing more than show up for church and drop a few dollars in the offering plate. Many churches recognize this problem and require candidates for membership to go through a formal membership process during which they are informed of the needs within the church that could be met by their gifts and talents. Thus the Membership Committee has the following responsibilities in the recruitment process:

1. *Interview Applicants*—As individuals on the Membership Committee interview applicants for membership, certain characteristics, talents, and areas of interest tend to emerge in the conversation. These impressions may then give the committee members opportunity to ask further questions.

2. *Information Regarding Past Service*—Indicators which may provide clues leading to the recruitment of new members as volunteer staff include the areas in which they have previously served both inside the church and in the community. A list of these experiences and any related training should be noted.

The fact that a person has served in a position does not necessarily indicate current interest. It is wise to ask the question, "Where do you see yourself ministering as a member of this congregation?" The question is broad enough to allow potential members to start a new direction in ministry or continue on a proven path of service.

3. *Forward Information to Pastor of Christian Education*—It is important that this informa-tion be fed as rapidly as possible to the person most knowledgeable about the recruitment process. Though there may be no immediate openings in the education program, the pastor of Christian education needs to begin the process of building a relationship with these new members in the areas of their interests and to assist them in developing their spiritual gifts.

Conclusion

It is obvious that the recruiting of volunteer staff in the local church is everyone's responsibility. But not everyone has the same responsibility. Just as the various gifts within the body of Christ complement each other to make a healthy and well-developed body, so the various functions within the recruitment process are necessary so the educational ministries of the church are adequately staffed at all times.

If the CE pastor has to do all the recruiting on his own, the job may never get done, or he might find himself so burned out and "people tired" that he will lose the joy and satisfaction of seeing people volunteer to serve.

With this larger picture in mind, we can go on to look at specific areas of recruitment and some of the tools which can be used to make recruitment of volunteers in the local church an effective and happy process.

P.S.: Some of this material was drawn from experiences of Christian education pastors and leaders with many years of effective service.

* * *

Pastor Herb Wilcox sipped his now cold coffee and shook his head. "Lord," he prayed, "if that young man you've sent me can handle something this complex, I am grateful. If he can't, please give him a hand. Amen. But—for me to use the pulpit to advertise his program— that's another story, Lord. I'll have to think about that one."

3

Recruitment Calendar: A Game Plan

The honeymoon was over. The first six months of Jeff's ministry had been an unexpected joy. The people of the Walnut Heights Bible Church had responded with enthusiasm to the creative ideas and spiritual insights of their resourceful young pastor of Christian education.

The Winter Institute of the Bible attended by 87 adults for four consecutive Wednesday nights in the freezing cold weather surprised even Pastor Wilcox. The Volunteer Ministry Recognition Dinner had been another well-received innovation. Abandoning the traditional potluck dinner in the church fellowship hall, for which members of the congregation showed little enthusiasm, Jeff persuaded three church businessmen to pick up the tab on a banquet at The Back Door, a restaurant specializing in juicy, tender prime rib. With the meal paid for, the church board had enthusiastically approved honorariums for Gerit and Sonja Connors, the president of the regional Sunday School association and his wife. Pastor Wilcox, Jeff, and Ernie Larson, chairman of the Christian Education Committee, thanked and encouraged the faithful band of volunteers for enthusiastically taking up the biblical challenge to serve. It was a wonderful conclusion to another year of ministry.

Other successes were in the works. Vacation Bible School was already staffed and organized with a week remaining before the public school year was to close. More registrations for summer day camp had poured in than any of the staff could remember. Even Winifred Doyle was pleased because Jeff himself had personally painted her classroom the pale sunshine yellow she had selected.

So, the honeymoon was over. All of these accomplishments were merely a prelude to the major organizational and recruiting tasks Jeff now faced. Already Thelma Packsma had resigned from the four- and five-year-old department because of summer plans. Gloria Benner, department leader of the junior teaching group, was expecting in July and did not intend to resume her responsibilities until the baby was out of diapers. That was only the tip of the iceberg.

Rick and Marian Fantozzi decided to move to Michigan; Johnny Banks returned to school; Henry and Debbie Forcash wanted to take a sabbatical after 11 years in the Junior High Department; and so the saga continued, seemingly with every ring of the phone. It was as if everyone had waited for the breaking in of the new pastor of Christian education to bail out en masse.

It was time for Jeff to develop and implement his game plan, preceded by a great deal of prayer. "With men it is impossible, but not with God," he found himself repeating, "for with God all things are possible."

The telephone was his deliverance. Calls were placed to seminary buddies, former professors, the Christian education director under whom he had interned, and four or five people who were only names on publicity pieces for Sunday School conferences. The phone seemed to become part of his ear as he asked repeatedly, "How in the world can I recruit all the volunteer staff I need for this summer and the coming school year?"

People talked. Ideas jelled. Bits and pieces began to come together.

Gradually a strategy developed—a game plan. The game plan wasn't perfect and had to be revised and amended from time to time, but at least it was a start on a systematic approach to recruiting volunteers. Gradually, Jeff began to feel it was going to work. The anxiety began to subside, and he told his wife, "I finally feel the Lord's giving me a handle on this job."

The calendar (pages 25-28) is a summary of Jeff's game plan. It isn't the plan Jeff implemented in those early months of ministry, but reflects the surviving elements of his strategy with the "wheat separated from the tares." (Later chapters will explain in detail how each element of the plan works.)

RECRUITMENT CALENDAR

PURPOSE

To outline a year-long, step-by-step approach to the recruitment of volunteer workers.

OUTLINE

September

1. Time and Talent Campaign (see chapter 4)
   a. Letters
   b. Brochure
   c. Publicity in bulletin and church newsletter
   d. Messages from pastor
   e. Service features during morning worship service focusing on specific ministries
2. Continue meeting with *ad hoc* recruitment group but conclude meetings by midmonth (see chapter 7).
3. Begin Teacher Aid Program (junior-high age training) and Teacher Aid Program for high schoolers who want to teach.
4. Promote training program
5. Follow up on registration cards (see chapter 5)
   a. Phone call
   b. Set up interview
   c. Ask to attend training program in fall
   d. Place in departments when appropriate
6. Follow up on new membership Ministry Questionnaires (see chapter 6)
7. Rhoda's Band (see chapter 8)

October

1. Time and Talent campaign (see chapter 4)
   a. Have faith promise responses put on computer printout.

   b. Have computer print address labels for each person who responds.
   c. Send letter of appreciation to each person not presently involved in the education program, asking them to call the Christian·education office for an interview with the Pastor of Christian Education.
   d. Phone all new volunteers who do not respond to the above letter (c.) and schedule appointments with the Pastor of Christian Education.
2. Follow up on registration cards (see chapter 5)
   a. Phone call
   b. Set up interview
   c. Direct to January training program
   d. Place in departments when appropriate
3. Follow up on new membership Ministry Questionnaires (see chapter 6)
   a. Set up interview
   b. Direct to January training program
   c. Place in departments when appropriate
4. Promote training program
5. Service feature on club program (see chapter 9)
6. Begin work on volunteer recognition dinner
   a. Establish means of paying for dinner
   b. Secure speaker

November

1. Follow up on registration cards (see chapter 5)
   a. Phone call
   b. Set up interview
   c. Direct to January training
   d. Place in departments when appropriate

2. Follow up on new membership "Ministry Questionnaires" (see chapter 6)
   a. Set up interview
   b. Direct to January training program
   c. Place in departments when appropriate
3. Feature church-time ministries in a bulletin feature and Sunday service interview (see chapter 9)
4. Service feature on early childhood ministries

December

1. Time and Talent campaign (see chapter 4)
   a. Complete appointments with new volunteers with Pastor of Christian Education.
   b. Send letter to all new volunteers and new members inviting them to attend an educational training program in January.
2. Follow up on registration cards (see chapter 5)
   a. Phone call
   b. Set up interview
   c. Direct to January training
   d. Place in departments when appropriate
3. Follow up on new membership Ministry Questionnaires (see chapter 6)
   a. Set up interview
   b. Direct to January training program
   c. Place in departments when appropriate

January

1. Hold educational training program for all volunteers and new members not already involved in the educational program.
2. Publicize educational training program (see chapter 9)
   a. Bulletin insert
   b. Church newsletter

c. Pulpit announcements
3. Follow up registration cards (see chapter 5)
   a. Phone call
   b. Set up interview
   c. Direct to April training
   d. Place in departments when appropriate
4. Follow up new membership Ministry Questionnaires (see chapter 6)
   a. Set up interview
   b. Direct to training program
   c. Place in departments when appropriate
5. Service feature on youth ministries
6. Establish committee to plan volunteer recognition dinner

February

1. Placement of newly trained volunteers (see chapter 10)
   a. Observation in departments
   b. Establish permanent substitute teachers for departments
   c. Place teachers where appropriate
2. Follow up on registration cards (see chapter 5)
   a. Phone call
   b. Set up interview
   c. Direct to April training program
   d. Place in departments when appropriate
3. Follow up on new membership "Ministry Questionnaires" (see chapter 6)
   a. Set up interview
   b. Direct to April training program
   c. Place in departments when appropriate
4. Select director for VBS and/or day camp
5. Service feature on children's ministries (see chapter 9)
6. Secure restaurant for volunteer recognition dinner

March

1. Prayer support month in Christian education (see chapter 8)
   a. Distribute prayer sheets to all adult classes on a weekly basis
   b. Use the services of the church to expose people to need for prayer support for the various educational ministries
      —joys
      —needs
      —requests
2. Follow up on registration cards (see chapter 5)
   a. Phone call
   b. Set up interview
   c. Direct to April training program
   d. Place in departments when appropriate
3. Follow up new membership Ministry Questionnaires (see chapter 6)
   a. Set up interview
   b. Direct to April training program
   c. Place in departments when appropriate
4. Summer staff recruitment
   a. Select departmental superintendents for VBS and/or day camp
   b. Send out letter to all volunteers from last year's VBS
5. Publicity on VBS and/or day camp
6. Rhoda's Band (see chapter 8)

April

1. Establish ad hoc recruitment group by midmonth (see chapter 7)
   a. Purpose: To recruit staff for summer and fall ministries
   b. Meet weekly with committee members for reports and assignments
   c. Interview all personnel recruited by committee
   d. Continue meeting until all positions are filled
2. Hold educational training program similar to that in January

3. Follow up on registration cards (see chapter 5)
   a. Phone call
   b. Set up interview
   c. Direct to April training program
   d. Place in departments when appropriate
4. Follow up on new membership Ministry Questionnaires (see chapter 6)
   a. Set up interview
   b. Direct to April training program
   c. Place in departments when appropriate
5. Recruit club leaders for all clubs
6. Send out Christian education evaluation letter to superintendents (see chapter 11)
7. Present Christian education media presentation in evening service (see chapter 9)
8. Complete plans for volunteer recognition dinner

May

1. Continue meeting with ad hoc recruitment group until positions are filled (see chapter 7)
2. Training program for club leaders
3. Follow up on registration cards (see chapter 5)
   a. Phone call
   b. Set up interview
   c. Ask to attend training program in fall
   d. Place in departments when appropriate
4. Follow up on new membership Ministry Questionnaires (see chapter 6)
   a. Set up interview
   b. Ask to attend training program in fall
   c. Place in departments when appropriate
5. Publicity on summer ministry
6. Training for VBS/day camp personnel
7. Hold volunteer appreciation dinner

June

1. Continue meeting with *ad hoc* recruitment group until positions are filled (see chapter 7)
2. Follow up on registration cards (see chapter 5)
   a. Phone call
   b. Set up interview
   c. Ask to attend training program in fall
   d. Place in departments when appropriate
3. Follow up on new membership Ministry Questionnaires (see chapter 6)
   a. Set up interview
   b. Ask to attend training program in fall
   c. Place in departments when appropriate
4. Rhoda's Band (see chapter 8)

July

1. Continue meeting with *ad hoc* recruitment group until positions are filled (see chapter 7)
2. Follow up on registration cards (see chapter 5)
   a. Phone call
   b. Set up interview
   c. Ask to attend training program in fall
   d. Place in departments when appropriate
3. Follow up on new membership Ministry Questionnaires (see chapter 6)
   a. Set up interview
   b. Ask to attend training program in fall
   c. Place in departments when appropriate

August

1. Continue meeting with *ad hoc* recruitment group until positions are filled (see chapter 7)
2. Publicity on recruitment (see chapter 9)
3. Service feature during morning worship service
4. Message(s) from pastor on ministry through Christian education (see chapter 2)
5. Follow up on registration cards (see chapter 5)
   a. Phone call
   b. Set up interview
   c. Ask to attend training program
   d. Place in departments when appropriate
6. Follow up on new membership Ministry Questionnaires (see chapter 6)
   a. Set up interview
   b. Ask to attend training program
   c. Place in departments when appropriate

4

Time and Talent Search

Jeff managed a quick "hello" to Peggy and ignored her look of surprise as he barged into Pastor Wilcox's office without knocking. She still was not used to the impetuousness of the former college athlete and big man on campus. Herb Wilcox, half-dozing in his swivel chair, sat up with a start, straightened his necktie and managed a patient if slightly annoyed smile. "What can I do for you, Jeff?" His voice held an edge of uncertainty, understandably evoked by his assistant pastor's brash entry.

"Pastor, I need your help—" Jeff began. "You know this Time and Talent Campaign we've been discussing, I think it would be great if you would kick it off from the pulpit."

Herb Wilcox took a deep breath and stared out his office window at the big broadleaf oak tree next to the nursery building. "I appreciate the energetic approach to your job, Jeff—I really do. But, you were hired to run the Christian education ministry, and I thought you were going to take the recruitment responsibilities off my back. Frankly, I can't see how that's being accomplished with you tossing the ball back to me."

Undismayed, Jeff pushed his glasses back onto his nose and continued. "Sir, it's just that the congregation needs to know you're behind it, that it's not some flash-in-the-pan idea I cooked up to see if we could get some nibblers to try it out. They need to know how important it is and why."

The senior pastor swiveled his chair around to face his young colleague. "Have you considered the possibility that the Sunday worship service might be too valuable in the spiritual feeding of the flock to sacrifice to a commercial or series of commercials for any special project?"

"Yes, sir—I have," Jeff said. "I know how they need to be fed, and I have a tremendous respect for your sermons. But they need to know more about feeding each other, too. All I ask is that you think about it, sir."

The problem, Jeff decided on his way home, was that his senior colleague of seven months didn't have an adequate understanding of what a Time and Talent Campaign was all about. To work right, it had to be a concentrated exposure of the congregation to biblical teaching about the use of natural talents and spiritual gifts in the local church. They needed to know there were varied opportunities for each person to make a commitment for service for the coming year.

Actually, there was a second more subtle problem. An inadequate understanding on the part of the church decision-makers of the biblical concept of every believer serving had caused the concept not to be emphasized in teaching. Though the Christian Education Committee had enthusiastically endorsed the Time and Talent Campaign, the church board had to appropriate the extra funds for printing and postage costs. They also would field the flack that was bound to come from the Harley Jenkins faction within the church for tampering with the morning worship service. Thus, Jeff had a low-key campaign to launch, starting with Pastor Wilcox and concluding with key members of the church board.

The minicrusade began with Jeff casually raising hypothetical questions in private conversations with Pastor Wilcox and—later—two influential board members:

"What needs do we have that are going unmet?"

"To what extent are these needs a result of insufficient personnel?"

"To what extent do you think our people are aware of the biblical teachings about stewardship as it applies to the use of time and talents as well as financial resources?"

"Do you think that biblically sound sermons on the subject would assist the board in ministering to the needs now going unmet?"

"Who would be the best person in the church to address these subjects?"

These questions obviously steered the discussion in a specific direction. In actual conversation, however, it wasn't so easy to toss them out so cleanly, or lay them end-to-end. But, each time Jeff was able to weave some of the questions into dialogues. In fact, his persistently suggesting Pastor Wilcox as the ideal voice to present these thoughts to the congregation tended to cement staff relationships and raise the board's opinion of their pastoral team. In a private meeting in his office, Pastor Wilcox told Jeff the idea was sound, and he would cooperate wholeheartedly.

The following month, the series of messages began, drawn from the gift passages in 1 Corinthians 12—14. Pastor Wilcox emphasized that every believer is gifted, and that every gift provided by the Holy Spirit is designed to be given away.

The Time and Talent series was well received by the congregation, and a respectable number of people began ministering within the church for the first time. However, as the pastoral team evaluated the response, two weaknesses became evident.

"The messages just weren't that practical," admitted Pastor Wilcox. "They were Bible-based but not well related to life—at least not the lives of our people." It was an honest confession—and he was right. The illustrations used were about other churches in different times. What was needed were current illustrations from the lifeblood of Walnut Heights Bible Church.

The second weakness was identified by Jeff's wife, Rita. "The girls in my Bible study group don't know how to respond to Pastor Herb's messages," commented Rita one night at the dinner table. "They're too fuzzy—too abstract. Most don't know what actual needs might be met through their services in the church. Some of the girls are feeling really guilty for not volunteering and frustrated because they don't know what they'd be volunteering for."

As Jeff thought about Rita's comment, the truth was apparent. He wasn't one to volunteer carte blanche for something that vague, either. He wanted a fairly clear picture of what was involved before he'd commit himself. How could he expect others to blindly go for something still so much up in the air?

From these two observations, a thoughtful, mature, and highly successful Time and Talent Campaign emerged the following year. Dynamic Sunday morning messages presented the biblical basis for Christian service while Sunday evening Pastor Wilcox laid out specific areas of ministry within the church fellowship. The following items proved to be the primary ingredients in the commitment drive:

1. Biblical messages, appropriately illustrated from the body life of Walnut Heights Bible Church, on a Theology of Service.

2. Personal testimonies from people who had experienced the joy of serving.

3. Slide features of ministries which deserved to be highlighted.

4. A list of all known service opportunities and who to contact for more information.

5. A commitment brochure printed and mailed to every person who attended the church during the previous year.

6. A definite Commitment Sunday, publicized well in advance, when commitment brochures would be collected and ministries would start functioning.

The following outline is a description of the Walnut Heights Time and Talent Commitment Campaign as it developed in the years that followed. Also included are samples of materials used to raise the awareness of the congregation in the area of use of talents in serving.

TIME AND TALENT COMMITMENT CAMPAIGN
Outline of Steps

WHEN?	BY WHOM?	WHAT?
During winter months	Church Board	• Examine and adopt the concept of a Time and Talent Commitment Campaign. • Adopt a theme for drive. • Establish a budget for drive. • Set dates for drive.
During spring months	Photographer	• Take color slides of the activities of the church in which volunteers participate (focus on close-up pictures—no more than two or three people in a picture). • Take similar black and white pictures which can be used in the brochure.
	Pastor of Christian Education	• Create a Time and Talent Commitment brochure and lay it out in rough copy. • Select a prayer chairman who will organize special prayer meetings for the actual dates of the Time and Talent Commitment Campaign.
Early summer	Editor: Church newsletter	• Announce dates of the Time and Talent Commitment Campaign in the fall (see page 29).
	Pastor of Christian Education	• Compile a list of known service opportunities in the church and the name of the person to contact for more information about those ministries (pages 35-38).
	Pastor	• Plan the major themes of messages. • Discuss themes with the pastor of Christian education to allow him to coordinate service features and testimonies with messages.
Late summer	Pastor	• Write a letter to the congregation which will introduce the Time and Talent Commitment Campaign and provide the brochure as a means of response (pages 41-43).
	Pastor of Christian Education	• Finalize brochure and have it printed. • Secure volunteers to stuff letters and brochures into envelopes. • Put together a slide-tape presentation (preferably programmed with two projectors and a dissolve unit) of volunteers in action to be used during the drive. • Select and contact volunteers from the previous year to testify of the joy of Christian service during the drive.

WHEN?	BY WHOM?	WHAT?
	Prayer Chairman	• Organize prayer groups and meeting times. (It is desirable to do this in conjunction with the existing structure within the church.)
Last week before drive	Pastor of Christian Education	• Mail letters from pastor to congregation. • Confirm various elements of drive. • Announce Time and Talent Commitment Campaign from the pulpit and through the bulletin. • Recruit volunteers to tabulate the commitment responses so that the information will be readily available throughout the rest of the year. (A computer printout may be quicker and more useful.) • Identify all unfilled volunteer ministry positions in the church. • Notify prayer chairman of existing ministry needs.
	Prayer Chairman	• Distribute information about existing ministry needs to prayer groups. • Distribute names of existing volunteers to prayer groups for praise and intercession.
During drive	Pastor	• Preach sermons on Time and Talent Commitment. • Use testimonies and slide presentations in the services.
	Pastor of Christian Education	• Distribute lists of known volunteer service opportunities. • Distribute additional Time and Talent Commitment brochures at the church services during the drive.
During drive	Prayer Chairman	• Keep in contact with all prayer groups and notify them of answers to prayer as volunteer ministry positions are filled.
	Editor: Church Newsletter	• Feature article on the Time and Talent Commitment Campaign (see page 34).
	Bulletin	• Insert one-page articles concerning service into the bulletin (see pages 45-47 for examples).
	Elders	• Collect commitment brochures on Commitment Sunday (the last Sunday).
First week after drive	Pastor	• Send form letters to people who responded, thanking them for their commitment to ministry. Two letters should be used, one going to those who are continuing in ministry and the other going to those who are new to volunteer ministry (see pages 52-53).

WHEN?	BY WHOM?	WHAT?
	Pastor of Christian Education	• Look through commitment brochures to discover people volunteering for ministries where help is needed immediately. • Set up interviews for each person who is new to the volunteer ministry of the church (see chapter 5). • Begin process of getting all of the responses listed (manually or by computer) according to the areas of ministry for which they volunteered (see pages 50-51).
Following weeks	Pastor of Christian Education	• Continue interview and placement process until all new volunteers have been placed or directed into more productive areas of ministry. • Notify current volunteer leadership (superintendents, head usher, club leaders, etc.) of volunteers for their areas of ministry.

_____

_____

_____

_____

_____

Walnut Heights Bible Church

2315 Walnut Road, Wheeling, IL 60090
— 312-555-1234 —

NEWSLETTER

Commitment Campaign Announced

"Hands of Time . . . and Eternity" is the theme of the Time and Talent Commitment Campaign scheduled for the last three weeks in September. The announcement was made by Board Chairman Jonathan Honeycut following the June board meeting.

The Time and Talent Commitment Campaign will include: (1) messages by Pastor Herb Wilcox related to the theme; (2) special prayer meetings asking the Lord to prepare the hearts of the congregation for a new year of service; (3) special features in the church services focusing on the various ways in which needs are being met through Walnut Heights Bible Church; and (4) a special service of commitment when each member and active attender of the church will be asked to present time and talents to the Lord.

"It is our aim," commented Pastor Wilcox, "to have every person in the congregation make a commitment of time and talent, no matter how great or small, for the coming year as a result of the "Hands of Time . . . and Eternity" Commitment Campaign.

Walnut Heights
Bible Church

Service
Opportunities

The number and variety of opportunities available at our church make it possible for everyone interested to find a nitch to use their time and talent in the Lord's service. Consider this list carefully and then contact the person designated as contact person in your area of interest.

A. Pastoral

—*Shepherding Ministries*—
Monthly contacts with an assigned group of people. Contacts may be made at church, at home, or on the telephone. Hospital visitation, and/or notifying pastors of individuals with needs.
Contact:

—*Adult Class Officer*—Elected positions in all Sunday School classes. Encouraging class members, planning events, choosing curriculum and planning the direction of the class in terms of teaching and support functions.
Contact:

—*Counseling: Lay/Certified*—If you possess a degree or experience in long-range counseling, the pastoral staff would be interested in possibly making referrals to you.
Contact:

B. Evangelistic

—*Jail Ministry*—Visiting inmates, leading Bible studies, counseling, encouraging men in the county jail.
Contact:

—*Neighborhood Bible Studies*—
Reaching out to neighbors through an evangelistic Bible study.
Contact:

—*2:7 Discipleship Training*—An opportunity to learn how to apply Christian principles in your life and pass them on to others..
Contact:

—*Church Visitor Visitation*—
Visit new people to our church in their homes and welcome them to Walnut Heights Bible Church.
Contact:

C. Teaching

—*Sunday School* (all ages)—
Always looking for new and additional teachers and substitutes. Commitment is on a yearly basis and curriculum is provided.
Contact:

—*High School Core Group Leaders*—Meet during the week with a small group of high school students and involve them in Bible study.
Contact:

—*Day Camp Counselors*—Day camp meets for 1-2 weeks each summer. Activities, Bible studies, missions, and taking trips to various places make up each day's activities. A counselor is in charge of a small group (up to 10) of children from one age-group.
Contact:

—*Awana Council-time Leader*—People who enjoy giving object lessons, and/or short talks to boys and girls. Age-level varies from K-8. Involvement varies from one week to two months.
Contact:

—*Women's Bible Studies*—There are many women's Bible studies meeting throughout the week. They are always looking for teachers who would be willing to come in for a specified time and lead their studies.
Contact:

D. Christian Education
(Administrative and Support Ministries)

—*Long-range planning*—Individuals with vision, educational insights, and knowledge in the area of planning.
Contact:

—*Christian Education Committee*—Meets monthly to establish policy, make and review decisions, and help determine direction for the CE program for all ages.
Contact:

—*Sunday School Department Leader*—Responsible for leading a group of teachers in working together in effective teaching of a specific group of children.
Contact:

—*Awana Club Director*—Same type responsibilities as above, except meets on Wednesday evenings under the Awana format.
Contact:

—*Sunday School Age-Group Coordinator*—Oversees and evaluates children's area Sunday School departments. Assists in recruitment of teachers and encourages leaders and teachers in their ministries.
Contact:

—*Day Camp Director/Assistant Director*—Works in planning the program, all parts and pieces of curriculum, and in training counselors and junior counselors.
Contact:

—*Media/Resource Center Technician or Worker*—Help keep the Media/Resource Center in good operating condition, help teachers find needed materials, be willing to try new mediums of expression for teaching, and discuss them with teachers.
Contact:

—*Missions Education*—Various opportunities for planning banquet programs and teaching children about world need.
Contact:

—*Librarian*—Assist in cataloging books, suggesting new books and services, serving as "check-out" librarian on Sundays.
Contact:

E. Counseling

—*Shepherding Ministries*—See letter "A."

—*Phone Shepherds*—Make telephone contact with new people who attend our church. Help answer their questions or refer them to someone who can. Training provided.
Contact:

—*High School Core Group Leader*—See letter "C."

—*Jail Ministry*—See letter "B."

—*Lay/Certified*—See letter "A."

F. Preaching

—*Rescue Mission Work*—Giving a Bible message to men and women on skid row.
Contact:

G. Children (Coaching and caring type ministries)

—*Sunday School*—See letter "C."

—*Quizzing*—Encouraging children to learn and memorize an entire book of the Bible each year. Compete with other teams from the area in answering questions on the material covered.
Contact:

—*Graded Choirs* (Primary 1 and 2, Middler 3 and 4, and Junior 5 and 6)—Pianists and directors.
Contact:

—*Nursery Worker*—Care for babies and toddlers during morning, evening, or Wednesday evening programs.
Contact:

Weekday child care during women's Bible studies
Contact:

—*Special Education*—Work with "special" children during the Sunday School hour.
Contact:

H. Youth

—*High School Core Group Leader*—See letter "C."

—*Summer/Spring Missions Project*—Go on a trip as a sponsor to various mission fields. Work with students in helping them to understand the meaning and significance of the missions activity in which they are involved.
Contact:

—*Junior High/High School Sunday School Teacher*—See letter "C."

—*Camp Counselor for Junior High or High School*—Same as counselor under letter "G."

—*College Ministries*—Teach a Sunday School class, lead and assist in a weekday Bible study. Invite college students into your home.
Contact:

I. Visitation

—*Cradle Roll Visitor*—Visit parents of newborn babies, give them literature, and find out if and where they are involved in our church.
Contact:

—*Outreach Leader in Sunday School*—See letter "B."

—*Transportation*—Often people in our congregation need rides to doctor's appointments, events, and church services.
Contact:

—*Work with the Elderly*—This could be many things from teaching crafts in the monthly meetings to bringing meals to a shut-in.
Contact:

J. Caring

—**Women's Prayer Groups**—There are several groups of women who gather weekly to pray for specific ministries in the church.
Contact:

—**Membership Committee**—Interview individuals who wish to join our church. Make phone contact with people who indicate interest in joining.
Contact:

—**Deacon/Deaconess**—See letter "A."

—**Transportation**—See letter "I."

—**Work with Elderly**—See letter "I."

—**Nursery Worker**—See letter "G."

—**Weekday child care**—See letter "G."

—**Office Help**—All kinds of office work: Collating, photocopying, typing, going over computer printouts, sorting church newsletter mailings, etc.
Contact:

—**Single Adult Ministries**—Being willing to help fix a car, repair something in a house, invite singles into your home for dinner and fellowship.
Contact:

—**Deaf Ministry**—Learn to sign, sign services, teach signing to others.
Contact:

K. Additional Opportunities that don't fit under existing headings

—**Stewardship and Finance Committees**—Financial and budget planning.
Contact:

—**Public Relations**—Writing news releases, planning promotion strategies, making posters, etc.
Contact:

—**Audio Committee**—Help operate the church sound system.
Contact:

—**Choir**
Contact:

—**Communion Committee**—Help set up for, and get elements ready for Communion observance.
Contact:

—**Social Committee**—Help set up punch, coffee, refreshments, various meals, for various social functions at church (i.e., annual meeting, Good Friday breakfast, mission banquets, going-away receptions, etc.).
Contact:

—**Greeters/Ushers**
Contact:

—**Cassette Ministry**—Duplicating tapes, recording, selling, etc.
Contact:

—**Assist in parking cars on Sunday mornings**
Contact:

—**Assist in snow removal**
Contact:

—**Senior High Handbell Choir**
Contact:

Walnut Heights
Bible Church

2315 Walnut Road, Wheeling, IL 60090
312-555-1234

Dear Friends:

A successful vacation, it has been said, is a period of relaxation when your self-winding watch runs down. Digital watches have nearly made the definition obsolete, but I trust that your busy summer has not made the idea of a vacation obsolete in your life. I hope you have been refreshed in your body and spirit.

With the summer vacation period coming to an end, it is our opportunity and responsibility as a church to set the hands of ministry in motion once again. Of course, many of these ministries have continued without losing a second during the summer, but now we need additional hands to keep up with the growth anticipated this fall.

Just before our Lord commissioned His 12 disciples and sent them out to minister (Matthew 10), He made one observation and instructed His followers to take one course of action. "The harvest is plentiful," He said, "but the workers are few. Therefore beseech the Lord of the harvest to send out workers into His harvest" (Matt. 9:37-38).

This is the most appropriate time of year for me to make a similar request of you, First, please *look* at the opportunities available to us as a church to meet needs in our community. Then *look* at your own gifts, abilities, and time commitments and ask yourself, "Where can I fit into ministry *this year?*"

Then *pray* that the "Lord of the harvest" will "thrust forth workers" to do His work in our community. Be assured that He does have the people to accomplish the ministries that He has in mind.

Our "HANDS OF TIME . . . AND ETERNITY" brochure accompanies this letter. It is designed to help you examine your time and talents and then make a year-long commitment to ministry in our community. Please look at it carefully and consider it prayerfully.

On the last Sunday morning of this month, please bring your "HANDS OF TIME . . . AND ETERNITY" brochure to church filled out as a commitment of your time and talent to the Lord. A special offering will be taken during the morning worship service at which time you will be able to present your time and talent as a living sacrifice to the Lord.

If you have any questions, please call me. May I assure you that I will be standing with you in prayer.

Sincerely,

Herb Wilcox

Herb Wilcox
Pastor
Walnut Heights Bible Church

HW/rb
Enc.

HANDS OF TIME...
AND ETERNITY

INSTRUCTIONS FOR COMPLETING THE TIME AND TALENT BROCHURE:

1. After prayerful consideration of God's Word and His leading in your life, complete this "Hands of Time . . . and Eternity" brochure.

2. Circle all numbers which describe the areas of ministry and the age/sex of people to whom you wish to minister.

3. Be sure to both sign and print your name, address, and phone number before returning the brochure on Commitment Sunday, September 25.

4. *Each person* should complete a "Hands of Time . . . and Eternity" brochure in order to distinguish among ministry preferences within families.

5. Tear off the front panel of the brochure, and transfer the areas of ministry that you have circled in the brochure to the panel which you have detached. Then post it in a location in your home where you will be reminded to pray for that ministry daily.

6. Bring the completed brochure to church or Sunday morning, September 25, and place it in the "Hands of Time . . . and Eternity" offering plate at the conclusion of the service as a celebration of your commitment to serve.

7. If you are unable to attend church on Commitment Sunday, please drop your brochure in the mail during the following week.

Thank you for your willingness to be used by God.

Walnut Heights Bible Church

2315 Walnut Road, Wheeling, IL 60090

312-555-1234

HANDS of TIME...
AND ETERNITY

Ours are the hands of time. Ours is the touch of eternity. The question that each of us at Walnut Heights Bible Church must ask ourselves as we consider the lives of people with whom we are in contact is as simple and yet complex as the lives we lead: "WHAT CAN I DO WITH MY TIME AND MY TALENTS TO HAVE AN ETERNAL IMPACT ON PEOPLE THIS YEAR?"

A time and talent commitment is one way to answer this question. God has graciously given us a growing church. Now we must be careful to commit ourselves to the ongoing ministry needs of our church and its worldwide outreach.

A time and talent commitment is:

. . .A *STEP OF FAITH*—Faith that God in His graciousness will see fit to accept our gifts and talents and use them for His glory.

. . .A *PROMISE TO SERVE*—Serve in a capacity compatible with our gifts and talents.

. . .A *CONFIDENCE OF BLESSINGS*—Blessings that only God can provide to those who are willing to say yes to His direction.

. . .AN *ANTICIPATION OF IMPACT*—Impact on people, young and old, rich and poor, sick and well, who need to be touched by the hand of God.

The Apostle Paul stated simply, "It is God who is at work in you, both to will and to work for his good purpose" (Phil. 2:13). As you examine the possibilities of service at Walnut Heights Bible Church this year, be assured that it is God who is guiding your desires and your pen as you write down your preferences for ministry in the coming year.

By God's Grace and under His guidance, I have committed myself to _____ ministries with _____ (age/sex) at Walnut Heights Bible Church during 1983-1984

Yes! I am interested in investing my time and talents in ministry . . . (Please circle the number that most closely describes the: A. *MINISTRIES* and B. *PREFERENCES* of the age and sex with which you would like to be involved.)

A. MINISTRIES

CARING MINISTRIES

Visitation
1111 Newcomers
1112 Telephone Visitation
1113 Shut-ins
1114 Sick
1115 Nursing Homes
1116 Hospitals

Special Assistance
1211 Elderly
1212 Handicapped
1213 Special Education
1214 Alcoholics
1215 Counseling
1216 Overnite Accommodations
1217 Cooking

WORSHIP MINISTRIES

Worship Services
2111 Usher
2112 Greeter
2113 Parking Lot Attendant
2114 Information Booth
2115 Nursery
2116 Sanctuary Decorations

Music
2211 Adult Choir
2212 Youth Choir
2213 Special Vocal Music
2214 Instrumental Music
2215 Song Leader
2216 Accompanist: Piano
2217 Accompanist: Organ
2218 Accompanist: Guitar

SUPPORT MINISTRIES

Administration
3111 Typing
3112 Filing
3113 Telephoning
3114 Assembling
3115 Bookkeeping
3116 Mailing
3117 Mimeographing

Communication
3211 Editor
3212 Writer
3213 Slide Presentations
3214 News Gatherer
3215 Photographer
3216 Paste-up
3217 Cassette Production
3218 Cassette Sales
3219 Proofreader
3220 Poster Maker
3221 Art Work

Transportation
3311 Youth Activities
3312 Special Events
3313 Van Available
3314 Station Wagon Available

Maintenance
3411 Landscaping
3412 Carpentry
3413 Cleaning
3414 Electrical
3415 Plumbing
3416 Painting
3417 Lawn Mowing
3418 Equipment Repair

Library
3511 Librarian
3512 Reviewing Books
3513 Cataloging
3514 Material Preparation
3515 Committee Member

Audiovisual
3611 Projectionist
3612 Filing
3613 Material Preparation
3614 Committee Member

DISCIPLING MINISTRIES

Sunday School/Children's Church
4111 Teacher
4112 Substitute Teacher
4113 Department Leader
4114 Department Secretary
4115 Children's Church Leader

Youth Work
4211 Sponsor
4212 Small Group Leader
4213 Home Available
4214 Pool Available
4215 Boat Available

Camping
4311 Resident Camp Director
4312 Resident Camp Counselor
4313 Family Camp Committee
4314 Stress Camp Leader
4315 Day Camp Director
4316 Day Camp Counselor

Club Program
4411 Boys Club Leader
4412 Girls Club Leader
4413 Committee Member
4414 Special Speaker

Specialized Ministries
4511 Vacation Bible School
4512 Christmas Program
4513 Drama
4514 Puppetry
4515 Refreshments
4516 Athletic Coach
4517 Family Life Committee
4518 Special Education
4519 Hearing Impaired
4520 Home Bible Study

MISSION MINISTRIES

Foreign Missions
5111 Missions Committee
5112 Correspondent
5113 Missions Conference
5114 Woman's Missionary Fellowship

Local Evangelism
5211 Neighborhood Bible Study
5212 Neighborhood Canvass
5213 Jail Ministries
5214 Outreach Projects
5215 Personal Work

B. PREFERENCE FOR MINISTRY

Age
6011 Preschool
6012 Grade School (K-6)
6013 Junior High (7-8)
6014 High School
6015 College/Career
6016 Adult—Married
6017 Adult—Single

Sex
6111 Male
6112 Female
6113 Male and Female

Name _____
Address _____
City _____ State _____ Zip _____
Home Phone _____
Business Phone _____

Your Signature _____

ALTERNATIVE TIME AND TALENT BROCHURE

WALNUT HEIGHTS BIBLE CHURCH

COMMITMENT CARD

Date_____19_____

NAME_____ BIRTHDAY_____

ADDRESS _____ Month   Day   Yr. (optional)

_____ HOME PHONE_____

CHURCH MEMBER_____PREVIOUS MEMBERSHIPS_____

CHURCH POSITIONS HELD IN PAST _____

CHURCH POSITIONS HELD AT PRESENT_____

OCCUPATION_____ WHERE EMPLOYED _____PHONE _____

PREVIOUS OCCUPATIONS _____

WHAT COLLEGE, OR PROFESSIONAL TRAINING HAVE YOU HAD? _____

_____

WHAT BIBLE, LEADERSHIP, OR TEACHER TRAINING HAVE YOU HAD? _____

_____

HOBBIES AND SKILLS _____

Personnel Committee Comments:

"HANDS OF TIME . . . AND ETERNITY"

You, Count on Me!

As a dedication of my time and talent for all Jesus Christ has done and is doing for me, I am willing to serve in one or more of the following ways (note code explanation at bottom of card):

SUNDAY SCHOOL
Regular Teacher — H I D T
Substitute Teacher — H I D T
Secretary — H I D T
Department Superintendent — H I D T
General Superintendent — H I D T
DVBS Teacher — H I D T
DVBS Dept. Superintendent — H I D T
DVBS Secretary — H I D T
Transportation — H I D T

CHILDREN'S CHURCH
Regular Teacher — H I D T
Substitute Teacher — H I D T
Department Superintendent — H I D T
Secretary — H I D T

TRAINING FELLOWSHIP
Children's Teacher — H I D T
Youth Sponsor — H I D T
Adult Officer — H I D T
Secretary — H I D T
General Supervision — H I D T

CLUB WORK
Boy's Brigade — H I D T
Pioneer Girls — H I D T
Other _____ — H I D T

MUSIC
Choir — H I D T
Part _____
Piano — H I D T
Organ — H I D T
Instrument
Type _____ — H I D T
Duet, Trio, etc. — H I D T
Solo — H I D T
Song Leading — H I D T
Direct Choir — H I D T
Choir Assistant — H I D T
Music Committee — H I D T

CLERICAL
Typing — H I D T
Addressing — H I D T
Keeping Records — H I D T
Folding and Filing — H I D T
Office Helper — H I D T

EVANGELISM
Evangelism Committee — H I D T
Personal Worker — H I D T
Jail, Hospital, Mission Teams — H I D T
Tract Distribution — H I D T
Visitation — H I D T
Child Evangelism — H I D T

CAMPS AND RECREATION
Camps and Recreation Comm. — H I D T
Camp Counselor — H I D T
Day Camps — H I D T
Recreation Director — H I D T
Ball Team Member — H I D T
Team Coach — H I D T
Pack Trips — H I D T
Other _____

VISITATION
Sunday School — H I D T
Sick and Shut-ins — H I D T
Membership — H I D T
Newcomers — H I D T
Community Census — H I D T
Cradle Roll — H I D T

AGE GROUP PREFERENCE
(as it relates to foregoing areas)
Nursery 0-3 — H I D T
Beginner 4-5 — H I D T
Primary 6-8 — H I D T
Junior 9-11 — H I D T
Junior High 12-13 — H I D T
High School 14-17 — H I D T
College 18-24 — H I D T
Adult 25- — H I D T

MISSIONS
Missions Committee — H I D T
Missions Correspondence — H I D T
Missions Projects — H I D T
Collect Missions Material — H I D T

MANUAL WORK
Kitchen Work — H I D T
Painting — H I D T
Carpentering — H I D T
Plumbing — H I D T
Electrical — H I D T
Yard Work — H I D T
Mechanical — H I D T
Custodian — H I D T

GENERAL
Bus Driver — H I D T
Church Publicity — H I D T
Decorating Church — H I D T
Flower Arranging — H I D T
Artwork — H I D T
Handcraft — H I D T
Photography — H I D T
Drama — H I D T
Library — H I D T
Audiovisual — H I D T
Trained Nurse — H I D T
Nursery Helper — H I D T
Church Newspaper — H I D T
Ushers — H I D T
Men's Fellowship Officer — H I D T
Women's Missionary Fellowship Officer — H I D T
WMF Circle Chairperson — H I D T

CODE: H—Have Done; I—Interested in Doing; D—Am Doing; T—Willing to take training. Circle the letter which indicates your experience, interest, or present participation.

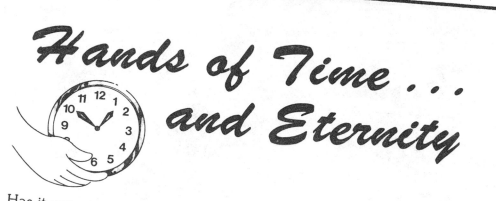

Hands of Time . . . and Eternity

Has it ever occurred to you what the digital watch is doing to our language? Phrases like "a quarter after 2" or "watch out for that boat approaching at 2 o'clock" will mean very little without the slow moving hands of a clock as a point of reference.

But even with digital watches, time still remains our most precious natural resource. The question each Christian must ask is, "What can I do with my time to make it count for eternity?"

Each of us has in our hand certain talents and gifts which can be used for God's glory. Each of us is limited by a multitude of demands on our time and energies. Thus each person in our church is encouraged to stop and ask himself/herself, "Where will my time and talents best be used for God during the coming year?"

In the "Hands of Time . . . and Eternity" Commitment brochure you will find five areas of ministry.

Caring Ministries put you in contact with people who are new to the church or need special care because of age, illness, or special circumstances.

Worship Ministries are related to the public services of the church.

Support Ministries refer to those essential tasks which take place behind the scenes without which communication, transportation, and maintenance would break down.

Discipling Ministries are the leadership opportunities for a person to have face to face contact with people who are willing to be taught the living and written truths of God.

Mission Ministries focus on the outreach of the church in the local community and around the world.

As you consider the opportunities presented in the brochure, please be in prayer that God will direct you in how you should use your hands for time and eternity.

Hide-and-Seek

Some people view service in a church as a game of home church hide-and-seek. With abilities ranging from acting, banner making, and carpentering to xylophone playing, yodeling, and zigzag stitching, they would enjoy having their talents used in the church but are afraid to let anyone know about their desires. Thus the game of hide-and-seek continues.

One of the disappointments of playing home church hide 'n seek is that frequently no one finds you. As a result, one begins asking all sorts of unrelated questions like "Don't they like me?" or "Am I not good enough for them?" or "Don't they need me?" The enjoyment of the game turns into frustration.

During our Time and Talent emphasis this month, we would like to introduce a new game. It is called Christians, Rise 'n Shine. The rules are simple. You submit your "Hands of Time . . . and Eternity" brochure on Commitment Sunday, September 25, to let the church know what you can or would like to do to build up the body of Christ (rise) and we will make every effort to insure that you can be used for God's glory in that capacity (shine).

Paul, in writing to the Ephesians, makes it clear that the pastor's responsibility is to equip the believers for the work of the ministry (Ephesians 4:12). Ministry in our church happens in church-time programs, at typewriters, on camping trips, under writing deadlines, over coffee, behind tape recorders, on top of changing tables, before plans have been made and after the last person has left.

This month we want to focus on the stewardship of you. We believe that God has given you to our church to minister to someone special. If you have not received the "Hands of Time . . . and Eternity" brochure in the mail, please pick one up in the narthex of the church. The easiest way for you to "rise" is to immediately fill out the form. Then bring it with you to church on Commitment Sunday. We will do our best to allow you to "shine" for the glory of God.

CARING ENOUGH TO DISCIPLE

In my hands are the names of people you may not recognize. They are very special people in that they are first-time visitors to Walnut Heights Bible Church. Week after week, new people drop by to see what we are like. Club meeting after club meeting new boys and girls are beginning to visit our weekday program. Many of them come to us with very little background in biblical teaching. Some have never discovered what it means to know Christ as their personal Saviour. But they come . . . and we gladly accept the responsibility to disciple them in the "grace and knowledge of our Lord Jesus Christ."

On an almost seven-day-a-week schedule, there are age-graded classes, elective classes, Bible studies, clubs or youth programs, adult classes, home Bible studies, and a host of ministries carefully designed to meet the spiritual and social needs of those who walk through our doors. We are committed to helping every new person find spiritual fellowship and maturity through the ministry of a loving, caring community of believers.

Obviously, this is only going to happen when those desiring to be discipled sit at the feet of "disciplers." Perhaps you have seen the poster which reads, "Don't Keep the Faith . . . Share It!" I believe that a significant key to unlocking the vast potential of the Walnut Heights Bible Church ministry could be the number of people who are consistently willing to be trained to "Share It!"

What does God really want us to do to bring new believers to spiritual maturity? What is our vision? How much time are we willing to spend to be trained in "making disciples of all men"?

You should have received a "Hands of Time . . . and Eternity" Commitment brochure in the mail. Additional brochures are available in the lobby of the church. You may have never served as a "discipler" before, but as you look at the brochure you'll discover an area of ministry that appeals to you. If you lack experience, sign up anyway. Then in large letters write the word "TRAINING" on the face of the commitment brochure. This will tell me that you want help getting started.

On Commitment Sunday, September 25, bring your "Hands of Time . . . and Eternity" brochure (with "TRAINING" written on it, if so desired) to the morning worship service. You will have the opportunity to begin the process which will lead you into a discipling ministry at Walnut Heights Bible Church.

Pastor Herb Wilcox

Walnut Heights Bible Church

2315 Walnut Road, Wheeling, IL 60090
312-555-1234

NEWSLETTER

COMMITMENT SUNDAY SET

Sunday, September 25, has been designated by the elders of Walnut Heights Bible Church as "Commitment Sunday." During the morning service, all members and regular attenders of the church will be called on to present their "Hands of Time . . . and Eternity" Commitment brochures as an act of worship and service.

In commenting on the nature of the service, Pastor Wilcox observed, "The objective is to experience a celebration of Christian service. The worship service will climax as each person places his/her commitment brochure in the offering plates passed by the elders of the church. The congregation will then rise to sing 'Lead On, O King Eternal,' and together dedicate itself to a year of Christian service."

The areas of service at Walnut Heights Bible Church include, but are not limited to, caring ministries, worship ministries, support ministries, discipling ministries, and mission ministries. "Hands of Time . . . and Eternity" Commitment brochures are available in the church bulletin, in the lobby of the church, and in the church office until Commitment Sunday.

INSTRUCTIONS ON HOW TO FOLLOW UP ON "HANDS OF TIME ... AND ETERNITY"

COMMITMENT RESPONSES

1. Recruit a group of volunteers to sort out the commitment brochures (or cards), placing the brochures of those already involved into one stack and those seeking to become involved into another stack.

2. Mail response letters to everyone who has responded—one letter to those who are already involved (p. 52) and another letter to those seeking to become involved (p. 53). These should be mailed within the week following Commitment Sunday.

3. Responses should be grouped according to the categories of response in order to have a handy reference list for recruitment purposes as needs arise. The easiest way is to have this done on computer (thus the numbers on the brochure). The alternative is a hand tabulation process (see page 60).

4. Distribute copies of the computer printout (or hand tabulation) to key people who will need the information for recruitment purposes during the year.

COMPUTER TABULATION

TABULATION SHEET
TIME AND TALENT COMMITMENTS

WALNUT HEIGHTS BIBLE CHURCH**

CHILDREN'S CHURCH LEADER—PRE-SCHOOL		SKILL LISTING	AS OF 07-APR-84	PAGE 35
000127-02 Ball*Carolyn**Mrs*		Home (312) 555-4321	Bus (312) 555-6789	[1] Level A
432 R——— Rd	Wheeling	IL 60090		
000133-02 Bucknel*Agnes**Mrs*		Home ( ) -	Bus ( ) -	Level A
334 F———	Prospect Heights	Il 60070		
000096-01 Cling*Stephen**Mr*		Home ( ) -	Bus ( ) -	Level A
805 D———	Wheeling	IL 60090		
000137-02 Cooper*Lura**Mrs*		Home ( ) -	Bus ( ) -	Level A
732 W———	Wheeling	IL 60090		
000142-02 Cunningham*Shirley**Mrs*		Home ( ) -	Bus ( ) -	Level A
1946 C——— Ln.	Wheeling	IL 60090		
000143-02 Ebersol*Terry**Mrs*		Home ( ) -	Bus ( ) -	Level A
618 L——— Ave.	Wheeling	IL 60090		
000013-02 Lawrence*Mary Anne**Mrs*		Home ( ) -	Bus ( ) -	Level A
533 W——— Ave	Buffalo Grove	IL 60090		
000023-02 Neighbor*Marjorie**Mrs*		Home ( ) -	Bus ( ) -	Level A
3S605 W——— Ave	Palatine	IL 60067		
000038-02 Peterson*Beth**Mrs*		Home ( ) -	Bus ( ) -	Level A
861 H———	Mt. Prospect	IL 60056		
000045-02 Smith*Nada**Mrs*		Home ( ) -	Bus ( ) -	Level A
413 W——— Dr	Wheeling	IL 60090		
000262-02 Taylor*Gail**Mrs*		Home ( ) -	Bus ( ) -	Level A
410 B——— Ct	Wheeling	IL 60090		
000262-01 Anderson*Delois***Mrs*		Home ( ) -	Bus ( ) -	Level B
210 P——— St	Wheeling	IL 60090		

[1] LEVEL REFERS TO PRESENT INVOLVEMENT: A = Presently active; B = Not presently involved

TABULATION SHEET
TIME AND TALENT COMMITMENTS

Year_____

INTEREST NUMBER_____

MINISTRY_____

	NAME	ADDRESS	PHONE NUMBER	PRESENT INVOLVEMENT
1.				
2.				
3.				
4.				
5.				
6.				
7.				
8.				
9.				
10.				
11.				
12.				
13.				
14.				
15.				
16.				
17.				
18.				

FOLLOW-UP LETTER to people presently involved.

Walnut Heights Bible Church

2315 Walnut Road, Wheeling, IL 60090
312-555-1234

Dear Co-worker:

Thank you so much for responding to the Time and Talent Commitment for Walnut Heights Bible Church. You were one of _____ people or families to so respond. Isn't it great to be among so many concerned people!

I realize that you are already involved in the ministry of our church in discipling people. Thank you for reconfirming your commitment. It means a lot to me.

Your brother,

Herb Wilcox

Herb Wilcox
Pastor
Walnut Heights Bible Church

HW/ma

FOLLOW-UP LETTER to people not presently involved.

Walnut Heights Bible Church

2315 Walnut Road, Wheeling, IL 60090
312-555-1234

Dear Steward of God's Time and Talent:

Thank you so much for responding to the ministry aspect of the stewardship program. You were one of _____ people to so respond. Isn't it great to be among so many concerned people?

The question now comes, "How do I turn my commitment into action?" Here are the steps you should take:

1. Since we prefer all new Christian education personnel to understand our philosophy of learning, we encourage you to attend our Christian Education Training Program which will begin on Sunday, October 9, at 9:30 A.M. in room 110.

2. We would like to interview you so we can get to know you more personally. Please call Pastor Jeff Thompson or me and set a time when we can get together.

3. Even though we may not be able to immediately place you in a ministry position, there are usually openings due to unforeseen circumstances after the first of the year. Please be patient in your willingness to serve. We will use you and your gifts as soon as possible.

Thank you so much for your response on Hands of Time . . . and Eternity Commitment Sunday. It means a lot to the leadership of the church to know that you are committed to serve Jesus Christ.

Your brother,

Herb Wilcox

Herb Wilcox
Pastor
Walnut Heights Bible Church

HW/rb

5

How Can I Volunteer?

"What does a person have to do in order to teach Sunday School around here?" blurted Rosemary Wilson to a rather stunned Jeff Thompson one Sunday after the morning service. He couldn't believe what he was hearing. In the first place, he would have never suspected that the shy, red-haired legal secretary would be interested in teaching Sunday School. Second, he'd never before seen Rosemary with sparks in her eyes and such animated gestures. It was obviously a case of blind bypassing of a potential recruit—a thought that brought a blush to his cheeks.

"Am I supposed to knock one of you pastors down and hold you there until you tell me I can work with those boys and girls? I've signed registration cards from the pew rack three different times, and nobody has ever bothered to contact me!"

"Well—consider yourself contacted," Jeff said, trying to pick up the ball. "I'm sorry, Rosemary. I honestly don't know why you haven't been called. But I will check on it."

Rosemary's mood mellowed and it appeared as if tears might well up in her eyes. "You can't imagine how difficult it is for a person like me to build up enough nerve to write a note to you, Pastor Jeff, much less ambush you after church. But I really do want to teach."

Jeff repeated his apology and made small talk with Rosemary, seeking further to help her feel needed.

"The registration cards," thought Jeff, after the Rosemary incident, "I wonder who looks at them after they're collected on Sunday mornings?"

A little checking turned up a procedure established somewhere back in antiquity in which the church secretary was responsible for looking at the cards on Monday morning. She then sent welcome letters to those who checked the "Visitor" box on their cards, sent Christian education fliers to those who checked the "Christian Education" box, and made a list of all the prayer requests and illnesses. The final step was to place a report of all this on Pastor Wilcox's desk for him to see Tuesday morning. The cards were then placed in a storage case and slipped into the cupboard above the mimeograph machine.

Jeff looked back through the registration cards over the past seven weeks, and sure enough, three times Rosemary Wilson's cards had two checks by the words "Christian Education." The first check was Rosemary's; the second, Jeff recognized, was the ink of the church secretary's pen. Three times she faithfully sent out the Christian education flier to an "obviously absentminded" parishioner, checking off the card indicating the follow-up had been done. The problem was, the list on Pastor Wilcox's desk—of potential Christian education workers—wasn't reaching Jeff.

Immediately the system was changed. On Tuesday mornings when Jeff walked into his office, a list of those indicating interest in Christian education awaited him, complete with phone numbers. Generally the phone calls required no more than 25 minutes to complete before he left the office at the end of the afternoon. True, most people merely wanted information about the Christian education program, but at least one or two every week wanted to become involved in the ministry to children, youth, or adults. A recruitment tool had been rediscovered, after almost remaining buried in an old bureaucratic ritual that wasn't making the right connections.

Out of curiosity, Jeff began logging his Tuesday phone calls (see log sheet on page 00). It wasn't long until an interesting trend began to emerge. A growing number of people whom Jeff had talked with on the phone were expressing appreciation to the young pastor for his warmth and helpfulness. Some of these, in turn, later began volunteering for the educational outreach ministry which touched so many lives for Christ. Courtesy had blossomed into a means of building up the very ministry that had generated seemingly fruitless initial inquiries. "Fruit needs time to ripen," Jeff realized. Courtesy and warmth had paid unexpected dividends.

In time the registration card was modified to make follow-up contacts easier to classify (see card on page 56) and more specific. Jeff soon discovered that he didn't need to make all the calls himself. A number of people from the church thoroughly enjoyed making this type of contact with people and were willing to accept the Tuesday follow-up as their primary ministry in the church. Log sheets were handed to Jeff by Wednesday night so he could be kept current with the contacts being made. Any person who could not be reached by phone got a letter on Thursday apologizing for not making phone contact, but expressing Jeff's desire to assist in any way possible if the person would give him a call at the church office (see letter on page 58).

Pastor Jeff had taken another step in meeting the needs of the recruitment problem. By not viewing people merely as potential workers, he'd gained rapport and established new relationships. From those relationships emerged a flow of individuals who wanted to join Jeff in the important CE ministry.

MODEL INFORMATION CARD—placed in pew racks

FRONT OF INFORMATION CARD

WELCOME TO OUR SERVICES

☐ a.m.
Date_____ ☐ p.m.

Mr. and Mrs.
Miss
Mrs. _____ Phone_____
Mr.

Address_____
Street   City   State   Zip
☐ This is a new address
Please check: AGE:
  ☐ Visitor   ☐ Regular Attender   ☐ Member   ☐ 12-17
  ☐ Desire information about _____   ☐ 18-22
  ☐ Desire to volunteer my time and talent   ☐ 23-30
  ☐ Desire church membership   ☐ 31-40
  ☐ Would like to receive a visit   ☐ 41-50
  ☐ Special request (see back of card)   ☐ 51-60
WALNUT HEIGHTS BIBLE CHURCH   ☐ Over 60

BACK OF INFORMATION CARD

Special request_____

_____

_____

Notes of information_____

_____

_____

Reservations desired for_____

_____

_____

FOLLOW-UP PHONE CALL
on "Desire to Volunteer" on Church Information Card

Ring, Ring

No answer, call again

Ring, ring ⟶ no answer (send letter)

"Hello, I'm Alice from Walnut Heights Bible Church, and I notice you marked that you want to volunteer your time and talent."

"Yes, that's right."

"Perhaps you could tell me a little of what interests you so I can put you in touch with the right people."

Left branch:

"I'm interested in _____"

"I've made a note of that and I am going to pass this information along to _____, and he will be in contact with you in the next few days."

"That will be fine. Thank you."

"Good-bye."

FOLLOW-UP ACTION
1. Name added to list of people whose names will be passed along to the appropriate person at the end of the day.
2. Information about follow-up call logged on church Registration Card Follow-up sheet.
3. Appropriate person contacted at end of day.

NEXT STEP ACTION IN RECRUITMENT FOR DISCIPLING MINISTRIES
1. Appropriate person follows up with a phone call and sets up an interview time and location.
2. Volunteer is interviewed using the Christian Education Interview sheet (see page 61).
3. Normal placement features are followed from this point on.

Center branch:

"I'm not sure. What kind of opportunities are there?"

"Actually we have opportunities for just about every interest, but we generally group them under five primary headings: (see Time and Talent brochure)
   Caring Ministries
   Worship Ministries
   Support Ministries
   Discipling Ministries
   Mission Ministries"

"Do any of these sound interesting to you?"

"What do you mean by _____ ministries?"

(Read from the Time and Talent brochure or the "Opportunities for Service" listing.)

"That sounds like what I'd like to do!"

"Good! I'm going to send some information to you on this ministry and a Time and Talent Commitment brochure so you can get the large picture of how you can volunteer."

"I would appreciate that . . . ."

"I am going to pass your name along to the person whose name I have circled on the "Opportunities for Service" list. He is a busy person, just like yourself, so if he doesn't call you within the week, why don't you give him a ring?"

"I'll follow your advice. Thank you."

"Good-bye."

Right branch:

"Oh, I misunderstood. What I really wanted was _____."

"It's all right, because I can give you that information as well" (see church bulletin and other resources for information).

"That's most helpful. Thank you for calling."

"You're so welcome. Good-bye."

FOLLOW-UP ACTION
1. Information about follow-up call logged on Church Registration Card Follow-up sheet.
2. No other follow-up may be necessary.

Bottom (merged from left and center branches):

FOLLOW-UP ACTION
1. Letter sent with "Opportunities for Service" list and Time and Talent Commitment brochure enclosed.
2. Name added to list of people whose names will be passed along to the appropriate person at the end of the day.
3. Information about follow-up call logged on Church Registration Card Follow-up sheet.
4. Give list of people called to the appropriate people via phone and then mail.

NEXT STEP ACTION IN RECRUITMENT FOR DISCIPLING MINISTRIES
1. Appropriate person follows up with a phone call and sets up an interview time and location.
2. Volunteer is interviewed using the Christian Education Interview sheet (see page 61).
3. Normal placement features are followed from this point on.

LETTER to people not successfully contacted in two phone call attempts.

Walnut Heights
Bible Church

2315 Walnut Road, Wheeling, IL 60090
312-555-1234

Mrs. Darlene Baltz
650 XYZ St.
Wheeling, IL 60090

Dear Darlene:
Thank you for your registration card indicating an interest in volunteering your time and talents. I'm sorry we were unable to reach you by phone.

Please call the church office at 555-1234; we will be glad to discuss your interest in serving the Lord or to answer any questions you may have.

Sincerely yours,

Jeff Thompson

Jeff Thompson
Pastor of Christian
Education

JT/rb

LETTER to persons wanting more information

Walnut Heights
Bible Church
2315 Walnut Road, Wheeling, IL 60090
312-555-1234

Mrs. Susan Johnson
221 ABC Drive
Wheeling, IL 60090

Dear Susan:

It was a joy to talk with you on the phone this morning. I trust that the information we discussed was helpful to you.

As I promised, I am enclosing two items: Our "Opportunities for Service" list and a Time and Talent Commitment brochure. I have passed your name along to the person whose name I have circled on the "Opportunities" sheet.

He is a busy person, like yourself. If he doesn't call you by the end of the week, please feel free to call him. His phone number is provided.

Thank you for your interest in serving the Lord.

Sincerely yours,

Alice Walker

Alice Walker
Volunteer Phone Visitation
Worker

CHURCH REGISTRATION CARD
FOLLOW-UP SHEET

Date	Name	Age	Address	Phone	Registration Card		Church Response	
					Item Checked	Information Provided	Contact Assigned	Results

CHRISTIAN EDUCATION INTERVIEW

Interviewee_____

Address_____
                                              City   Zip

Phone (Home) _____ (Work) _____

1. Background Information: (What has contributed to making you who you are today?)

2. Spiritual Life: (If you would die tonight, what kind of reception would you receive from God?)

3. Experience in Christian education: (What have you done to teach people about Jesus Christ?)

4. Area of Interest: (What types of ministry would you like to have this year?)

5. Greatest Apprehension: (What do you fear most about volunteering as you have?)

6. Desired Reward: (What personal satisfaction or rewards would you like to receive for ministering this year?)

Assignment _____ Date Available_____
Comments:

Interviewer _____ Date_____

6

Expectations of New Members

It was a 10-minute drive from Jeff's house to the church. This December morning he barely noticed four filling stations, two bowling alleys, and five traffic signals as he drove along. A thought had occurred to Jeff as he approached the two elm trees whose dark leafless silhouettes marked the two-mile point on his jogging route earlier that crisp winter morning.

Simply stated, the idea was this: "If we can give a packet of offering envelopes to new members of the church, why can't they be given a packet of service cards as well? After all, hadn't Pastor Wilcox made a strong point during the Time and Talent Commitment emphasis during October that stewardship encompassed not only financial aspects of the Christian life but the use of one's gifts and abilities as well?"

The longer the idea lingered on his mind, the more exciting the concept became. By the fourth traffic signal, Jeff had the packet visualized. The box would be approximately the same size as the packet of offering envelopes, but the contents would be significantly different. The first item would be a tape of Pastor Wilcox's most moving sermon from the Time and Talent series preached during the fall. Also included on the tape could be testimonies from volunteers featured during that same period in the fall and the touching words spoken by Alice Clarkson as she received the Walnut Heights Bible Church Sunday School Teacher of the Year Award at the Volunteer Ministry Recognition Dinner the previous May.

Next would come a set of ministry cards—one for each area of ministry of the church.

They could be drawn from the list of opportunities for service developed during the fall (pages 35-38), and could include a brief description of the ministry plus the name and telephone number of the person to contact for more information. These could be printed individually in case one of the ministries was later dropped or changed. Then the whole list would not have to be reprinted—just that particular card.

In a separate color, a Ministry Experience Questionnaire could be included. The purpose of the MEQ would be to record the ministry background of each new member of the church. The questionnaire, as Jeff visualized it, would contain a checklist of formal training and seminars in areas related to Christian ministry, talents and skills, and a record of ministry experiences enjoyed over the years. No one would be forced to submit this to the church, just as new members were not forced to tithe. However, Jeff hoped every fresh batch of membership candidates would consider options and responsibilities for service along with the other privileges of church membership.

The last piece in the packet would be a preaddressed and prepaid Volunteer Service Commitment Card, a scaled down version of the Time and Talent Commitment brochure used during the fall. Each new member would be encouraged to fill out the card and drop it into the mail within a week after he or she had received the right hand of fellowship. Then these responses would be added to the list of volunteers tabulated after the Commitment Campaign held during the fall.

Jeff fairly exploded into Pastor Wilcox's

office, still wondering if that last traffic light had been red or green. The ideas came pouring out of him like water from a rainspout. Pastor Wilcox peered unimpressed at Jeff over the rims of his granny glasses. "Slow down, Jeff," he sighed. "If it's all that good, it will stand up to slower sifting. I like some of what I hear, but—" Jeff reddened impatiently. He should have realized by now that any of his creative brainstorms if presented too hastily and excitedly would meet with initial caution from his senior pastor. Pastor Wilcox had developed a response that Jeff learned to interpret as a cold-water treatment, or "slow-down-Mr. Hotshot." The pastor would blandly say something like, "Oh, that's nice," which left Jeff wondering if he should drop the whole idea.

Undeterred, Jeff bided his time. At an opportune moment, two weeks after first sharing the idea, he brought it up again in a much more composed fashion. This time Pastor Wilcox seemed much more open. But there remained a distinct lack of enthusiasm for the idea which Jeff could not understand.

In his attempt to sort out why the senior pastor appeared to be dragging his feet on this potentially dynamite innovation, Jeff had lunch with Ernie Larson, the stocky, balding chairman of the Christian Education Committee. Ernie wore the loudest neckties Jeff had ever seen—but he was also one of the most perceptive and discerning men in church leadership.

"Could it be finances?" asked the chairman, after hearing Jeff out.

"No," responded Jeff, "if we get our printing done by Fred Cowan at Master Graphics (who had volunteered during the Time and Talent Commitment Campaign the previous fall) and the tape duplication through the church's cassette ministry people, the total cost to get the idea rolling would be under $100. Besides, the pastor has assured me that money won't be an issue on an otherwise good idea."

"How about the board?" the chairman continued. "Is Herb getting flack from them over your volume of innovations?"

"Negative again. I've raised that question with him several times in the last three months, and his feelings seem to be that almost every idea I bring up makes him look good for having recruited me."

"Maybe we should break down the problem into its component parts," Ernie suggested. "Let's see if we can discover where the holdup might be."

For the next half hour the two men picked over the details of Jeff's bogged-down brainchild. Almost all its main elements were timely retreads of ideas that Walnut Heights had already used, not really controversial. "What about the tape with the pastor's message?" Ernie queried.

Jeff shook his head. "That's Pastor Wilcox at his best," he said. "Why would he object to his own taped sermon?"

"I remember that message," the chairman said. "Maybe you're overselling it, in terms of your enthusiasm for the whole project. Is it really *that* good, Jeff? Would Herb think it was all *that* good?"

"You might have something there." Jeff let his mind go back to the fall Time and Talent series. "I remember Pastor Wilcox telling me how rushed he felt putting those sermons together on such short notice. Come to think of it, he really didn't come across very enthusiastically. And he forgot to mention ..." Jeff reddened. "You're right, Ernie. We talked about the series later. I guess I was his worst critic, since it was my idea. And he agreed that he'd needed more time to work out the ideas.

"Pastor Wilcox must think I'm an amnesia case for not remembering my own criticisms! How could I have been so insensitive?"

In October the following year, after an outstanding series of messages delivered by Pastor Wilcox on the subject of the Theology of Service, a Volunteer Service Packet was introduced, acquainting new members with service opportunities they had as parishioners in Walnut Heights Bible Church. A tape was included.

VOLUNTEER SERVICE PACKET

1. CASSETTE TAPE

"HANDS OF TIME ... AND ETERNITY"
REV. HERBERT WILCOX
WALNUT HEIGHTS BIBLE CHURCH

2. MINISTRY CARDS

MISSIONARY OUTREACH MINISTRIES

MUSIC MINISTRIES

SINGLE ADULT MINISTRIES

HIGH SCHOOL YOUTH GROUP

GIRLS CLUB MINISTRIES

BOYS CLUB MINISTRIES

SUNDAY SCHOOL MINISTRIES

MINISTRY EXPERIENCE QUESTIONNAIRE

NAME_____ PHONE_____
ADDRESS_____ CITY_____ STATE_____ZIP_____

WHAT SKILLS AND TALENTS DO YOU HAVE WHICH COULD BE USED AT WHBC?
_____

WHAT TRAINING HAVE YOU HAD WHICH MIGHT ASSIST YOU IN MINISTRY AT WHBC?
_____

WHAT EXPERIEN AT WHBC?
_____
_____

IN WHAT AREA LIKE MORE
_____
_____

3. MINISTRY EXPERIENCE QUESTIONNAIRE

VOLUNTEER SERVICE COMMITMENT CARD

AS A NEW MEMBER OF WALNUT HEIGHTS BIBLE CHURCH, I UNDERSTAND THAT I HAVE THE PRIVILEGE AND RESPONSIBILITY OF COMMITTING MY TIME AND TALENTS TO SERVE IN THE MINISTRIES OF THE CHURCH.

AFTER REVIEWING THE SERVICE OPPORTUNITIES PROVIDED IN THIS PACKET, I WOULD LIKE TO MAKE A COMMITMENT TO SERVE IN THE FOLLOWING CAPACITIES:

_____
_____
_____

SIGNED,

WALNUT HEIGHTS BIBLE CHURCH

4. VOLUNTEER SERVICE COMMITMENT CARD

MINISTRY CARDS

1. SUGGESTED FORMAT:

TITLE OF MINISTRY:

Description of Ministry:

Schedule of Meetings:

Leadership Needed:

Person to Contact for More Information:

WALNUT HEIGHTS BIBLE CHURCH 2315 Walnut Road, Wheeling, IL 60090
312-555-1234

2. FORMAT ILLUSTRATED:

SUNDAY SCHOOL MINISTRIES/CHILDREN'S CHURCH MINISTRIES

Description: Each Sunday morning educational opportunities are provided from the cradle to the grave as human needs are focused on through the lense of the Bible. A map Is provided on the back of this card in order to show class locations.

Schedule:
  9:30 Sunday School (all ages)
  11:00 Children's Church (through second grade)
  7:00 Third Wednesday night of month—Staff Planning/Training Meeting

Leadership Needed:

Department Leaders	Song Leaders
Teachers	General Officers
Secretaries	Adult Class Officers
Pianists	Visitors

Person to Contact for More Information:
  Rev. Jeff Thompson (555-1234)

WALNUT HEIGHTS BIBLE CHURCH 2315 Walnut Road, Wheeling, IL 60090
312-555-1234

MINISTRY EXPERIENCE QUESTIONNAIRE

FRONT OF CARD

MINISTRY EXPERIENCE QUESTIONNAIRE

Name_____ Phone_____

Address_____

City   State   Zip

Answer each of these questions as fully as you feel comfortable.

1. What skills and talents do you have which might be used at Walnut Heights Bible Church?

_____

_____

_____

- -

(Fold to make 3″ x 5″ card)

2. What training have you had which might assist you in ministry at Walnut Heights Bible Church?

_____

_____

_____

3. What experiences have you had which might assist you in ministry at Walnut Heights Bible Church?

_____

_____

_____

4. In what areas of ministry would you be most likely to serve during the coming year?

_____

_____

_____

- -

(Fold to make 3″ x 5″ card)

5. If you could do anything for God without fear of failure, what would that be?

_____

_____

_____

_____

_____

WALNUT HEIGHTS BIBLE CHURCH 2315 Walnut Road, Wheeling, IL 60090
312-555-1234

VOLUNTEER SERVICE PACKET (continued)

VOLUNTEER SERVICE COMMITMENT CARD

As a new member of Walnut Heights Bible Church, I understand that I have the privilege and responsibility of committing my time and talents to serve in the ministries of the church.

After reviewing the service opportunities provided in this packet, I would like to make a commitment to serve in the following capacities:

_____

_____

_____

Signed,_____

WALNUT HEIGHTS BIBLE CHURCH 2315 Walnut Road, Wheeling, IL 60090
312-555-1234

7

Recruitment Group

"Growth is a problem, not just an opportunity," concluded Roy Mayfield, a slender retired schoolteacher and one of the age-group coordinators with whom Jeff was meeting.* A blessing, they all agreed, but yet a problem just the same.

The four age-group coordinators huddled with Jeff in his office as the sounds and scents of late spring drifted in through his partially opened windows. Several years had passed since the first Time and Talent Recruitment Campaign, and even with the success of the fall recruitment efforts, it had become increasingly evident that something else had to be done in the spring and summer months to keep the ministry fully staffed.

"It seems to me," continued Jo, the grade school children's Sunday School coordinator, "that all we should have to do is get enough information to the people of our church for them to see the need and then respond. Our people have shown a real commitment to evangelism and discipleship. All they need is information."

A questioning look crept across Mary Ellen's freckled face. For two years now this tireless auburn-haired housewife had served as the early childhood coordinator for the church-time ministries, and consistently her area of ministry had been the first to need replacements but the last to be staffed. At first she blamed herself. But as time passed and the same pattern repeated itself a second time, her fellow coordinators helped her see that she was doing everything the rest of them were in just as tactful and compelling a manner, yet with less satisfactory results.

"Maybe prayer is the key," Mary Ellen offered wistfully, half questioning and half commenting. "All the information in the world won't necessarily bear fruit without the prayer support of God's people. The verse about praying the Lord of the harvest to send forth workers into the harvest fields keeps coming to mind. That doesn't just apply to missionaries in West Irian. It's equally true right here in Wheeling."

For the next few minutes the discussion focused on reasons why people attending Walnut Heights Bible Church *should* be volunteering to minister to the new families who had been added to the Sunday School roles in the last few months and what the biblical norms were in the early church. Yet the fact remained: departments were short of staff.

"What we need is revival," concluded Mary Ellen. "There's nothing else we can do except pray for it."

"Revival?" Jeff half mumbled. The very idea resurrected thoughts of his childhood in the rural South where "revivals" began on Sunday and concluded the following Sunday. That memory was a far cry from the idea of revival which Mary Ellen had been referring to, but the word had stimulated a brand new train of thought.

"Revival," pondered Jeff, as the conversation continued around him. What *had* brought about certain periods of deepening spiritual insights and commitment during his child-

---

*An age-group coordinator is a person assigned to assist the pastor of Christian education in the recruiting, training, and encouraging of teachers and department leaders in either Sunday School or church-time at a particular age-level (early childhood, children, youth, or adult).

hood? Later, at Young Life ranch, what were the common denominators that linked the spiritual responses of high school students in Colorado with the denominational evangelism in a neighboring community? Was it emotion? Prayer? Oratorical skills? Suddenly the fog cleared in Jeff's overactive mind. A pattern emerged.

"The fact is," interjected the young pastor, as if he had been totally immersed in the conversation the entire time, "that we've tried each of the concepts that *should* have worked, and they have to a great extent. But, we're still short of volunteer staff. Perhaps the problem is that we're using these ideas piecemeal fashion instead of pulling them all together.

"The word 'revival,' which Mary Ellen referred to a few minutes ago," Jeff continued, "triggered some thoughts in my mind. Each spiritual awakening I know of combined the two elements we've mentioned plus one other. Prayer followed by Bible-based information and an invitation to commitment. It's in response to an invitation that people make decisions."

Suddenly, everyone was talking at once about how years ago such invitations were commonly given in evangelistic services, tent revivals, and church camps. "They still do it in many churches," Jo offered excitedly. "But some groups have learned to personalize it. Young Life, Campus Crusade for Christ, and Campus Life get into one-to-one discussions where the evangelist first earns the right to be heard, then shares the Good News with the person and asks for a decision for Christ."

"Where are you going with all of this?" interrupted Mary Ellen, impatiently.

Jeff grinned. "I think we should use the same pattern in our recruitment efforts. After specific prayer about who should be contacted and who should do the contacting, let's seek out people who have 'earned the right to be heard' by virtue of their ministry within the church, and ask them to evangelize on behalf of our ministry needs, one on one with other church members, then ask for specific responses —decisions."

Mary Ellen brightened and they all broke into spontaneous applause. The air of gloom vanished. A sense of excitement emerged as the five members of the leadership team refined the basic concept and hammered out a new recruitment strategy to help them deal with the spring personnel shortage.

From that discussion in Jeff's office emerged what came to be known as the Ad Hoc Recruitment Group. "Ad Hoc" was used to indicate the temporary nature of the group, for it would be brought together only when recruitment needs outran available volunteers and regular leadership couldn't come up with more.

The following procedures were developed, which proved their value repeatedly in subsequent years:

Daily Prayer

Jeff and his age-group coordinators prayed specifically for the best people to work as members of the ad hoc recruitment group. Then after the recruitment group was in place, continued in daily prayer for the specific ministry needs of the church.

Group Selection

After a potential group had been formed, Jeff would contact each person individually. Though each was approached in a manner consistent with how well Jeff knew the person, three steps emerged as normal procedures: a contact letter, a job description, and a personal discussion (usually on the phone).

Recruiter's Notebook

The easiest method for the members of the group to keep themselves organized and on top of task was to have all the information they needed together in one place. So Jeff developed a notebook which was given to each member of the recruitment group, which was updated on a weekly basis. The book included:

1. A list of all ministry positions available.
2. The names of the people who had already committed themselves to ministry during the coming year or for the interim.
3. Ad Hoc Recruitment Group Report sheets to be used to log and report contacts.
4. Job descriptions for each of the ministry positions in the church.
5. A list of the people in the congregation

along with their addresses, telephone numbers, and Sunday School class affiliations.

Weekly Breakfast

One of the most memorable traditions which emerged from the ad hoc recruitment group was the Saturday breakfast at a local restaurant. This particular time was chosen because most of the mothers in the group could call for "reinforcements" at home on Saturday morning, then they could slip out for an hour with a minimum of disruption to the family's schedule. Most of the group members enjoyed having breakfast together (at their own expense) away from the distractions of family and phone.

Normal Schedule

Soon the breakfast meeting became a very comfortable routine. Breakfast and fellowship were followed by a brief prayertime (yes, even at the back table of a busy restaurant). Reports would follow, with Jeff asking each person to comment on conversations with each individual assigned to group members at the previous breakfast meeting. Discussion concerning the remaining ministry openings came next, as Jeff updated his co-workers on the progress of ministry commitments and then focused on suggestions for the best people to approach to take responsibility for the remaining opportunities. Usually Jeff had some specific names in mind before breakfast, but invariably new names were tossed in which had never occurred to him. The breakfast would conclude after six to eight names were assigned to each group member for contact during the coming week.

Personal Contact

During the coming week, each group member was responsible for making the assigned contacts at his or her own convenience. The conversation usually included a warm greeting which identified the caller with Walnut Heights Bible Church, a transition statement about the opportunities for Christian service available during the coming year, and a personal invitation: "Where do you think you would like to minister in the church during the coming year?" The direct question (invitation) was the key to the whole process. Without it the process would, for the most part, fizzle, ending in a noncommittal "I'm just not sure." With it, each person contacted had prompting and encouragement to examine his or her own gifts, talents, and abilities and to zero in on an appropriate target ministry for the coming year.

From this point on, Jeff would follow the normal procedures for interviewing and placement of volunteer workers. But now there was a special group whose sole function was to support the work of Christian education, the age-group coordinators, department leaders, and others within the church by obtaining new volunteers to assist in ministry.

COMMITTEE MEMBER CONTACT LETTER

Walnut Heights
Bible Church

2315 Walnut Road, Wheeling, IL 60090
312-555-1234

June 14, 1984

Mrs. Carolyn White
318 W_____ St.
Wheeling, Illinois 60090

Dear Carolyn:

I am sitting here staring at a stack of recruitment needs which we have both immediately and for this coming fall. For an optimist, this stack is quite a challenge. For a pessimist, the same stack is overwhelming. I must confess that I am an incurable optimist and so I believe we are going to be able to meet our recruitment needs.

Even the greatest optimist cannot do a job such as this by himself. For that reason, I'm writing to ask if you could work with me in an *ad hoc* recruitment group which will meet weekly through at least October. It will be the task of this group to contact by phone key people in the church, asking them to staff various positions in the education program. I am enclosing a job description of what we will need to do.

There is a very urgent need for our church, and I need capable people to serve with me in this crucial period of recruitment.

I will be in my office at 10:30 this Sunday morning. Please drop by and let me know if you would be able to serve with me.

Sincerely yours,

Jeff Thompson

Jeff Thompson
Pastor of Christian Education

JT/rb

AD HOC RECRUITMENT GROUP

1984

WALNUT HEIGHTS BIBLE CHURCH

PURPOSE

1. To recruit a full staff of Christian education workers for positions beginning September 4, (198___).
2. To contact the people of our church (via phone or in person) in order to discover where they feel their gifts can best be used.

PROCEDURE

1. Pray every day for the right people to minister through the educational department of the church. The Lord will supply.
2. Meet with the group for breakfast once a week until either October 1 or the staff is recruited, whichever comes first.
3. Each person will be assigned to contact about eight people per week.
4. In contacting the people assigned:
   a. Ask where they would be interested in serving the Lord in the Christian education program this year.
   b. Inform them of the anticipated areas of need.
   c. Set up a tentative appointment with them on a Friday afternoon or a Saturday for interviews and answer any questions.
5. Report back to the group concerning the responses of the people contacted.

SUNDAY SCHOOL
and CHILDREN'S CHURCH
Ministry Positions and Personnel
Walnut Heights Bible Church

CRIB NURSERY   9:30 A.M.
1.

2.

3.

4.

5.
TODDLER DEPARTMENT
(12-24 mo.)   9:30
1.

2.

3.

4.
2-3-YEAR-OLD
DEPARTMENT   9:30
1.

2.

3.

4.
4-5-YEAR-OLD
DEPARTMENT   9:30
1.

2.

3.

4.
1ST-2ND-GRADE
DEPARTMENT   9:30

CRIB NURSERY   11:00 A.M.
1.

2.

3.

4.

5.
TODDLER DEPARTMENT
(12-24 mo.)   11:00
1.

2.

3.

4.
2-3-YEAR-OLD CHURCH   11:00
1.

2.

3.

4.
4-5-YEAR-OLD CHURCH   11:00
1.

2.

3.

4.
1ST-2ND-GRADE
CHURCH   11:00

CHRISTIAN EDUCATION
AD HOC
RECRUITMENT GROUP

Report Sheet — Week of _____

Date	Name	Address	Phone	Personal Information	Interest Area	Contact	Results

WALNUT HEIGHTS BIBLE CHURCH
Christian Education Department
Job Description

1. Title: Department Leader
2. Length of Service: One year or until August 31 (whichever comes first). Commitment will be reevaluated at that time.
3. Basic Function:
   Responsible for supervising/evaluating/supporting the staff and program of department. Guides both teachers and students to ensure effective Bible learning.
4. Sunday Morning Responsibilities:
   A. Coordinates room setup and supplies.
   B. Greets members/visitors.
   C. Assigns/guides visitors to classes.
   D. Assists teachers as needed.
   E. Leads department large group.
   F. Keeps time schedule
   G. Observes/evaluates department staff to note problems/improvements
   H. Affirms, supports department staff
5. Team Responsibilities:
   A. Works with Sunday School administration (age-level coordinator and director of children's ministries) in:
      —enlisting/training new staff
      —training current staff
      —recommending/securing adequate facilities, equipment
      —recommending/implementing a department organizational plan with the proper teacher/learner ratio and department size to facilitate learner involvement
   B. Organizes and leads regular department training/planning meetings
      Leads Department in:
      —planning, conducting, evaluating its work
      —evaluating/planning units and lessons
      —setting goals for improvement and evaluating progress
      —planning outreach into the community
      —planning/implementing follow-up strategies for both visitors and members
   C. Assists/supports teachers by:
      —modeling effective teaching skills
      —encouraging use of new Bible learning methods and practice of new teaching skills
      —encouraging teachers to express honestly their crit-

icism, suggestions, ideas, feelings
—encouraging teachers in their own spiritual growth
—assisting teachers to guide involvement learning in small groups
—being available to assist with needs, problems
6. Other Responsibilities:
   A. Acts as liaison between department staff and Sunday School administration
   B. Is required to attend one training conference sanctioned by the Christian Education Department each year.
7. Time Commitment Responsibilities: Most well-prepared department leaders will spend a minimum of four-six hours each week in preparation and classtime.

WALNUT HEIGHTS BIBLE CHURCH
Christian Education Department
Job Description

1. Title: Teacher
2. Length of Service: one year or until August 31 (whichever comes first). Commitment will be reevaluated at that time.
3. Basic Function: Responsible for creating an effective learning environment and guiding/involving learners in life-changing Bible learning.
4. Reporting Responsibilities: To the department leader who is responsible for the efficient and effective functioning of the entire department's team.
5. Sunday Morning Responsibilities:
   A. Works with department team in setting up room to create an effective learning environment.
   B. Is ready to greet first learner who arrives and to involve him/her in meaningful participation.
   C. Guides Bible learning by:
      —selecting challenging Bible learning methods/activities
      —helping learners explore and discover God's truths
      —being well-prepared in the use of Bible stories, verses/passages, questions, comments (as appropriate to age-level) that help to accomplish the Bible teaching/learning aim
      —encouraging learners to be honest in expressing their ideas and feelings
      —helping learners apply Bible truths in ways that result in changed lives
   D. Evaluates learners' progress.
   E. Models the love of Christ and the power of God's Word in his/her own life in ways that are appropriate to the age-level.
   F. Shows love and concern for learners by getting to know them, accepting them where they are, actively listening to them and sharing their concerns/needs/joys.
   G. Affirms, supports learners.
   H. Keeps to time schedule worked out by department team.
   I. Participates with learners in large-group time and assists department leader as needed.
   J. Follows up on absentees.
6. Additional Responsibilities:
   A. Participates regularly in department training/planning meetings.
   B. Is required to attend one training conference sanctioned by the Christian Education Department each year.
7. Time Commitment Responsibilities: Most well-prepared teachers will spend a minimum of three-five hours each week in preparation and classtime.

LIST OF
ADULT CLASS MEMBERS

Class Name _____

Age Range of Class Members _____

Number Enrolled _____

Role	Name	Address	City	Zip	Home Phone	Business Phone	Sex	Information

8

Prayer Support

Mary Ellen's comment kept ringing in Jeff's mind:

"The verse about praying the Lord of the harvest to thrust forth workers into the harvest field," she had said, "doesn't just apply to missionaries in West Irian. It's equally true of the children right here in Wheeling."

There were people in the church whose primary ministry was in the area of prayer. The men's prayer group, for instance, met every Saturday morning in the prayer room behind the sanctuary to bring before the Lord the needs of the church and to support the missionary family in intercessory prayer.

Miriam Kowalski, homebound due to age and frail physical condition, was one of the church's strongest prayer warriors. Undaunted by her afflictions, Miriam's prayer life had only been enhanced by her advancing age. Old-timers at the church claimed that she'd single-handedly prayed the Campbells and at least a half a dozen other boys into the ministry during her years in Walnut Heights Bible Church.

There were other prayer groups as well. Most were small. Most were linked to a common age, interest, or cause such as the high school group, an adult Sunday School class, the Women's Missionary Society, and the Sunday School department leaders who prayed together at their monthly meetings. These were groups already meeting for prayer, and, with proper information consistently channeled to them, they could become intercessors for the volunteer needs of the entire church.

Phone calls were made to those Jeff knew in each of these prayer groups. Each time the response was approximately the same, "No, we haven't been praying for volunteers to serve within the church mainly because we didn't know what the needs were."

Two methods of communicating ministry personnel needs to the prayer groups were set up. By each Wednesday, Jeff would put into the mail a current list of ministry needs as well as an update on the prayers that had been answered. The lists would also be distributed at the midweek prayer meeting so everyone could also participate in the recruitment process through prayer at home.

In case any group wanted to know more about ministry needs so prayers could be more specific, they would need to call someone for more information. Ordinarily, Jeff would have been happy to become the phone contact, but he was already overcommitted. It would be necessary to find another volunteer to fill the slot. Jeff knew just the right person. He picked up his phone and dialed.

"I'll do it!" Mary Ellen Watkins agreed. It seemed to be a case of the right person for the right job. After all, it was Mary Ellen's problem that had initiated this whole process of seeking prayer support. Now, not only would the early childhood coordinator's program be brought to the Lord's attention, but other program needs as well.

The system was ready to go. Jeff and Mary Ellen would review the needs each Sunday. Then the prayer group leaders would call during the week to be kept current with recruitment needs and answers to prayer. "It's very exciting," reported Mary Ellen, after the system was underway. "Those calls can become miniature revivals as we rejoice over what the

Lord is doing in our church. It almost seems a shame that the children, who benefit the most from the new teachers and club leaders, are not actively involved in the prayers that the Lord is answering so beautifully. That's where the fun and action are!"

Again a light went on in Jeff's mind. Why shouldn't the younger members of the body of Christ be part of the exciting prayer life of the church? After all, wasn't it Rhoda, a young girl at the prayer meeting in John Mark's house in Acts 12, who roused the saints to rejoice over the fact that their prayers had been answered and that Peter, miraculously freed from prison, was standing at the gate outside? Of course children should be part of the recruitment prayer process!

Yet, children are different. For one thing, a child's attention span is significantly shorter than that of an adult. Another factor is that a child perceives needs directly connected with his own realm of experience much more easily than remotely related needs. Consequently, to pray for a teacher for his sister's Sunday School class would mean more to a second-grader than to pray for a chairman for the missionary committee of the church.

With these thoughts in mind, Rhoda's Band was formed for grade-school children in Sunday School. Three times a year—fall, spring, and summer—just before day camp (or whenever the needs arose), Rhoda's Band was called into action as one of the early arrival activities. Each edition of the Band lasted four weeks. The first week emphasized to the children the need for Rhoda's Band:

1. Pray *daily* that the Lord would provide *His* teachers and club leaders for ministry positions with which the children had contact.
2. Encourage adults (especially Mom and Dad) to pray with him or her for the Lord to meet that need.
3. Report back during the early arrival activity time as to how often the need had been prayed for by him or her and by others.

The remaining three weeks would then be spent hearing reports from the children about their faithfulness in praying the Lord of the harvest to send forth workers into their harvest field, reporting to the children concerning the people God provided in answer to their prayers and praying together that God would meet these needs. Sometimes the members of Rhoda's Band were encouraged to write postcards to the people who had responded in answer to their prayers. Then new prayer assignments were made. Each new edition of Rhoda's Band never lasted more than four weeks so the idea wouldn't become trite or stale to the children.

At this point, prayer not only met recruitment needs, but had become a teaching tool. Children and adults alike were beginning to discover and delight in the faithfulness of God as He responded to prayers which Jesus Himself had commanded His followers to pray.

Walnut Heights
Bible Church

2315 Walnut Road, Wheeling, IL 60090
312-555-1234

Dear Brother or Sister,

I don't like being this impersonal but I have an urgent request to pass along to you.

I need your help mobilizing people to *pray* for volunteer workers at Walnut Heights Bible Church. You can do this by:

1. Getting the people in your class or department to pray *every day* for the needed staff. You can aid this process by distributing the recruitment prayer sheet that you will receive this week.

2. Pray *publicly* for the needs of the department each week.

Enclosed is an outline of our strategy to mobilize prayer support in our church. Mary Ellen Watkins, our recruitment prayer coordinator, will be in contact with you to answer any questions you may have about this vital prayer responsibility.

Your brother,

Jeff Thompson

Jeff Thompson
Pastor of Christian Education

JT/rb
Enc.

RECRUITMENT PRAYER SUPPORT STRATEGY
Walnut Heights Bible Church

Where we are:
1. For the past three years we have done nearly everything we could to recruit Christian education staff, including well over 400 phone calls, pleas from the pulpit, following up on stewardship responses, etc.
2. At the same time Sunday School has grown in attendance.
3. Consequently, we find ourselves constantly short of Christian education workers.

Where we should go:
1. Since it is the Lord's responsibility to thrust forth workers into this field of service (as to all fields), we must be involved in asking Him to provide workers.
2. We must continue doing everything possible to recruit Christian education staff while realizing that only God can provide them for His work.
3. We must mobilize as many people as possible to pray for the Christian education staff and their ministries.

What we will do:
1. Contact the following groups of people and ask them to pray *daily* for the staff needs of Christian education:
   - Church Board
   - Officers of Adult Classes
   - Church Prayer Chain
   - Sunday School Teachers
   - Church-time Teachers
   - Club Leaders
   - High School Mom's Prayer Group
   - Wednesday Night Prayer Meeting
   - Weekly Women's Prayer Meetings
   - Women's Missionary Fellowship Prayer Circles
   - Saturday Morning Men's Prayer Group
2. Update the recruitment prayer requests by means of the Volunteer Staff Needs sheet by Wednesday and distribute to all of the above.
3. Questions about the personnel needs or concerning the activities of people to be recruited should be directed to Mary Ellen Watkins, the recruitment prayer coordinator.
4. Teach children to pray by creating Rhoda's Band—an early arrival activity for Sunday School children.

WEEKLY LISTING OF NEEDS

VOLUNTEER STAFF NEEDS
Walnut Heights Bible Church

Week of _____

"Pray ye the Lord of the harvest that He will thrust forth laborers" (Luke 10:2).

Immediate Needs:

	No. Weeks Listed	Prayers Answered
SUNDAY SCHOOL (9:30 A.M.)		
_____		
_____		
_____		
_____		
_____		
CHILDREN'S CHURCH (10:45 A.M.)		
_____		
_____		
_____		
CLUBS		
_____		
_____		
OTHER NEEDS		
_____		
_____		
_____		

This sheet is to inform you of our education needs. Please keep them in mind as you pray each day.

RHODA'S BAND INSTRUCTION SHEET
Walnut Heights Bible Church

PURPOSE
1. To teach children to pray that the Lord of the harvest would "send out workers into His harvest" (Matt. 9:38).
2. To obtain volunteer workers for the ministry of the church partially as a result of the prayers of children.

AGE-GROUP
Rhoda's Band of prayer warriors will be comprised of children in the third through sixth grades.

MEETING TIME AND LOCATION
At 9:15 A.M. on Sunday mornings in the Middler and Junior departments of Sunday School, for four weeks in a row, at three different times this year:
1. September 4, 11, 18, 25
2. January 8, 15, 22, 29
3. June 3, 10, 17, 24

LEADERSHIP
1. Mary Ellen Watkins will serve as the coordinator of Rhoda's Band and will be responsible to provide membership cards, prayer requests, and answers to prayer to the various Rhoda's Band leaders just prior to and during the dates listed above.
2. Middler and Junior Department leaders will appoint one teacher to be the Rhoda's Band leader in their departments.

PROCEDURE
1. Rhoda's Band leaders will announce and explain Rhoda's Band one week prior to previously listed dates, encouraging children to join.
2. On the first Sunday the leader will meet with children 15 minutes prior to Sunday School and briefly tell the story of Rhoda's participation in prayer over adults' concerns (i.e., Peter), tell the needs for volunteer workers in the church, explain responsibilities of Rhoda's Band members (see membership card), and distribute membership cards.
3. On the following three weeks the leader will receive reports of prayer activity from children (five minutes), tell of answers to prayer and new needs (five minutes), pray for newly stated and not-yet-answered prayers (five minutes).

RHODA'S BAND
MEMBER IN GOOD STANDING
As a member of Rhoda's Band (Acts 12:12-14), I promise to:
1. Pray *every day* that God would give excellent adults to lead our Sunday School, Children's Church, and clubs.
2. Encourage my friends (including adults) to join with me in prayer for adult leaders.
3. Report to my Rhoda's Band leader on Sunday mornings for three weeks in a row about how I prayed for adult leaders.

_____ _____
Rhoda's Band Leader's Signature   Student's Signature

9

Publicity

There are some things a person does almost instinctively. Publicity was one of those areas for Jeff Thompson. Perhaps that's why his conversation over lunch at the regional Sunday School association meeting had seemed so unusual.

The conversation was triggered almost incidentally after a workshop on leadership development. As Jeff was leaving the room with four other fellows, one of them threw out to his colleagues what seemed to be a simple question.

"What do you fellows do to promote Christian education ministries in your churches?"

The question seemed straightforward enough, and Jeff waited for the others to start tossing answers to the man. No one spoke. Each person seemed to be waiting for his companions to open up first with ideas, insights, methods tested in the fire of experience. But the only sounds in those few seconds were their own footsteps on the gleaming hallway floor.

"We've tried a few approaches," Jeff finally volunteered. "They might seem old hat to you but they've worked at our church."

As the group made its way to a nearby restaurant, the assistant pastor from Walnut Heights Bible Church shared his experiences and ideas about publicity as well as why he used each method of promotion. The response of the group surprised Jeff. His thoughts had seemed so simple, so logical, so obvious. Yet the ideas appeared refreshingly new to his colleagues.

"Pastor Thompson," said one of his new friends, "I think you're the one to do the workshop presentation on publicity and re-cruiting at next year's regional Sunday School association meeting." Jeff was too surprised to respond.

The Christian education pastor from Walnut Heights Bible Church had refined the random hash of ideas he'd shared with a few colleagues the previous year and packaged them in a logical progression he felt would make sense to pastors with or without experience in the areas covered. The word had apparently made its way through the grapevine; over 40 pastors and Christian education directors were present.

PUBLICITY AND RECRUITMENT WORKSHOP

The purpose for providing publicity as a part of the recruitment process is to maintain a high visibility for the ministries in which volunteers participate. Publicity stimulates and sustains a high level of motivation and interest on the part of congregation members in being involved. This includes the removal of false impressions or information.

PRINCIPLES

1. *Keep the joy and responsibility before people.* The focus of each piece of literature or public statement about volunteer service should be positive and based on the mandates of Scripture. Guilt and other forms of manipulation are not acceptable as tools for securing workers. Such approaches are not scriptural, and they are counterproductive over the long run. The emphasis should be placed on sharing our gifts and talents with others in anticipation of the joy

with which the Holy Spirit rewards those who are faithful and obedient.

2. *Publicize often.* Look for ways to place information about ministry before the people of the church. Don't wait for routine times such as late summer and early fall, when members of the congregation are anticipating recruitment plugs and may have developed a built-in resistance to the content of what is being said. Instead, publicize Christian education throughout the year, reporting frequently on what the Lord has been doing. At Walnut Heights Bible Church the senior pastor and the pastor of Christian education sit down together at least once a year to plan times during each month when visibility can be provided for the educational ministries of the church in one or more of the following: morning services, evening services, bulletins, church newsletters, quarterly business meetings, and church board meetings.

3. *Prepare carefully.* Don't waste the time of the congregation with useless clichés and ill-prepared announcements. Respect the integrity of your people by putting as much time and care per minute of delivery into public announcements as your pastor places in the preparation and delivery of his sermons. This will allow people to gain confidence in the ministry before they make commitments to serve.

4. *Visualize meaningful elements.* If one picture is worth 1,000 words, one well-chosen illustration is worth at least 500 words. Statements convey knowledge whereas illustrations communicate feelings which frequently "hook" the motivational instincts of the listener. Testimonies of changed lives are perhaps the best source of meaningful illustrations.

5. *Use a variety of voices.* Though the pastor will usually be the most effective spokesman for recruitment purposes, even his influence will be diminished by overexposure. The pastor of Christian education, the education committee chairman, Sunday School superintendent, and club leaders might be other voices as long as they are gifted, or trained in basic communication skills. The mere fact of their positions, however, doesn't automatically "qualify" them to bring visibility messages before the congregation. In fact, unofficial and unexpected voices might be more effective at times. One pastor of a very large church invited his early childhood workers to bring one entire preschool department into the morning worship service during the announcement time and interviewed a couple of the children before putting in a plug for teachers of the department.

6. *Piggyback on success.* The best time to enlist new staff for ministry is immediately after God has accomplished some exciting results through service in the church. But this type of enlistment will not take place unless the people of the church know what's been happening. Tell them. Then ask for new volunteers. Church camp, rally day, high school ministry projects, and special family activities can serve as launching pads for renewed awareness of ministry potential.

POSSIBILITIES

In addition to the normal means of "making announcements" about ministry opportunities, the following methods should be considered:

1. *Interviews*—An interview can be rehearsed, and this may give effective, but shy volunteers the confidence to share what God has been doing through them.

2. *Testimony*—In many churches testimonies of meaningful service are spontaneously shared within the time normally allowed for testimonies or body life experiences. Planned sharing in worship services is also effective.

3. *Skits or dramatic vignettes*—This means of communication is best when it is carefully planned and tied into a theme that is being developed elsewhere in the service.

4. *Slides*—Close-up pictures (no more than two or three people in each picture) can easily be shown in church services to illustrate the types of ministries which are happening at the church; they can also be used with a rear projection device in the front lobby of the church to visualize the ongoing ministries of the church.

5. *Video cassettes*—A video cassette tape player can be placed in the lobby of the church once a month in order to highlight some of the ministry activities of the church during the preceding month.

6. *Media presentations*—Sometimes equipment can be rented or borrowed from a school district or community college which will allow a person to program a tape with narrative,

music, and sound effects which can be synchronized with two slide projectors to provide a dramatic, exciting "show-and-tell" presentation communicating the joys of service.

7. *Movies*—From time to time Christian films featuring the Sunday School or other avenues of ministry in the local church can be shown as part of the church service.

8. *Ministry bulletin board*—One large display area in a highly visible location and changed on a regular basis can become a focal point for honoring special people, posting pictures, displaying awards, and featuring ministry needs. Take time to do a beautiful, creative job.

9. *Pins and name tags*—Some means of identifying those already involved in ministry serves as a reminder to other people in the church that they, too, may become involved.

10. *Posters*—Either the original or purchased variety can reinforce the message that everyone needs to be involved in service. (Don't leave the same posters up longer than two weeks; they quickly lose impact.)

11. *Opportunity sheets*—These can be attractively typed up and distributed periodically through the adult Sunday School classes.

12. *Bulletin announcements*—Though this is often the first means that we use to recruit volunteer ministers, it should be used in harmony with the many other methods of publicity.

Parable

Once upon a time, on the edge of a large and barren desert, lay a village whose people were ragged and hungry. What few crops they could grow were soon used to feed their many children. The goats were thin and devoid of life-giving milk. Life was desperate.

That August was becoming a month of death. The normal rainy season had not come, except for widely scattered showers. The grass was brown. Animals lay dying. The cries of hungry children were constantly in the air . . . until the stranger drove into the village.

No one seemed to know where he came from or why he selected their village. All they knew was that on August 25 the stranger drove into town in a truck loaded with food, water, and some very peculiar looking equipment. Wherever he saw children (and there were many), he would stop and give them water and a little food. Then the stranger would give a box of food to the parents of each child and say, "I have no more food to give you—but I know a way you can get all the food you need. Come to my truck tonight, and I'll explain."

Curiosity built up. By evening, every father in the village was standing around the stranger's truck. The question they asked was the same. "How can we get that much food?" Carefully, the stranger unloaded the equipment from his truck and patiently began explaining how the people could produce food, even on the edge of a great desert. For three years the stranger stayed, working day and night to train the people of the village in the skills of desert farming.

Soon the village became a thriving city. People came from near and far to enjoy the benefits of the community. Men trained the boys of the community just as the stranger had trained them. Women taught the girls to grind the grain into meal and flour for bread. The people of the village were well-fed and happy.

In time, the people began taking their prosperity for granted. They didn't like the work it took to maintain the machinery. Adults thought it a waste of time to train the younger generation to use the equipment properly. Instead they preferred to enjoy lectures on equipment use, crop processing, and how to market their products.

Eventually, the older generation died, and the younger generation found that they could not operate the machinery or produce the crops. Gradually, the people of the village found themselves becoming ragged and hungry. Many wondered why.

For more information on the village, please contact the church office.

Recruitment Countdown

As of the writing of this bulletin feature, the Christian education ministry has a variety of staff needs. These are perhaps greater than any needs we have experienced in the past year.

Why, I am asked, do we have this urgent need at this time? I think we can isolate at least a half-dozen reasons:

The Armed Services Effect—Just as servicemen expect to be rewarded if they "volunteer," many others in our society have become conditioned to volunteer only if they do not have to sacrifice anything (fun, social times, leisure).

Loneliness—Many people feel lost and without deep relationships in our suburban society. Thus, they fear that if they have to serve in Sunday School or children's church, they will lose contact with the few friends they now have.

Continuing Education—The adult classes of the Christian education program bring support and helpful instruction to many adults who feel that leaving their adult classes to teach children will hinder their own personal development.

Working Women—It used to be that men could expect their wives to handle all of the teaching load because they had time to prepare. With the growing number of working women in the church, men are going to have to stop passing the buck and shoulder their share of the teaching load.

Passion Gap—Many people have ceased to believe that boys and girls need to be led into a personal relationship with Christ. Of course, no one says this, but the absence of this passion is evident by our lack of sufficient teachers.

Big Church Myth—"If they need me, they will call me." Or, "There are so many people at our church, I'm sure they do not need me." These and other big church myths keep many from volunteering.

Can you identify with any of these reasons for not becoming involved? I would like to help you deal with any of these negative feelings you may have with regard to teaching. Please take a registration card. Fill it out and indicate if you would like to talk to me about your role in the educational ministry of our church.

10

Interviewing and Placing Teachers

Some lessons are learned the hard way. Like saying no to a person who is convinced that God is calling him to teach fourth-grade boys when that very class has been without a teacher for nearly a month.

Jeff had been the pastor of Christian education at Walnut Heights Bible Church for only a little over a year when a fascinating situation arose. Harry Van Horn had been transferred to Atlanta, leaving an opening in the teaching team that spring. For three weeks after Harry's departure, the class was juggled around between substitute teachers and combined classes. "I've tried my best to find a replacement," the department leader told Jeff. "I really feel bad about those kids."

"You aren't alone," Jeff replied. "I've asked seven people to consider taking over that position. They all said no. We really need to lift this up in prayer."

Then Marshall Burlington appeared. Actually, a telephone call brought the first contact between Jeff and the middle-aged salesman who had moved into the community just nine months before.

"I feel the Lord has called me to teach those junior-age boys," Marshall told Jeff after briefly identifying himself.

A miracle! thought Jeff. *I can't believe the way the Lord is taking care of this need!*

"How did you find out about the opening?" the pastor of Christian education queried. The recruitment process had been carried out without public announcement in order to avoid getting the overzealous/underqualified applicants that can become a thorn in the side of any Sunday School department.

"The Lord just told me to call you," the salesman responded, "so I figured there had to be an opening."

Who can argue with God?

The next Sunday, despite some feelings of apprehension on Jeff's part, the young pastor met his enthusiastic new middle-aged, slightly balding recruit outside the Sunday School office at 9:05, reviewed briefly the requirements for teachers that they had discussed on the phone, gave Marshall the teaching materials, and took him to the fourth-grade class to observe. Why the apprehension? Jeff wondered. Marshall Burlington seemed pleasant enough, and it appeared obvious that the Lord had provided this new teacher for a very teachable group of boys.

The following week Marshall Burlington began teaching. Within three weeks it was obvious that the department was in trouble. The salesman-turned-teacher was loud, aggressive, and always showed up poorly prepared. Each lesson somehow ended up in hammering the doctrine of sovereign grace into the boys, no matter what the text was or what the lesson aims were scheduled to be. It wasn't that the doctrine was heresy, it was simply not synchronized with the Sunday School program for that age-level or in harmony with the rest of the teaching staff.

Fortunately, for the Walnut Heights Sunday School, the problem was solved without conflict three months later when "Gracie" Burlington (as he had come to be called by his 10-year-old students) was transferred to a new territory by his company. Once again the teaching position was open, but this time Pastor

Jeff decided to be more careful in his interview and placement procedures.

In the days that followed, Jeff pulled together, for reasons obvious to all, a set of standard procedures for interviewing and placing workers. Guidelines for these procedures were:

1. Interviewers will insure that only qualified people are selected for ministries requiring specific gifts, talents, skills, aptitudes, and training.
2. Each candidate will be evaluated in terms of whether he/she will harmonize with other members of the assigned teaching team.
3. Interviewers should tactfully attempt to identify areas in which training or skill development would be helpful.
4. Care must be taken to insure that the ministry expectations of the new volunteer can and will be met.

Invariably, one of these guidelines became the basis for a bonding between volunteer and pastor. Later, as Jeff developed age-group coordinators, they too found the process to be helpful in building strong ties between themselves and their volunteers.

The procedures were established as follows:

1. Recruitment interviews will be done *face to face* and *in private.* Telephone interviews or discussions in crowded hallways seldom allow for accurate perceptions of the volunteer. Nonverbal clues may be missed. Follow-up questions may not be asked because of uncertainty over who else might be listening to the conversation. Besides, if the person does not have the time to set aside for the personal interview, there is a good possibility that he or she will not find enough time to tend to other aspects of the ministry responsibilities.

2. Recruitment interviews will follow a *standard format.* This information will be written down and retained in a notebook or file for future reference, but it will also provide the initial basis for determining the readiness of a person to accept leadership responsibility. Seven areas of information will be included:

Testimony—Describe your relationship with the Lord and where you are in your Christian walk today.

Training—What type of classes and seminars have you taken which have sharpened your ministry skills in the areas of your interest? What (if any) books, tapes, and films or videotapes have been the most useful to you?

Experience—What experience have you had in ministry? (Even though the person may wish to move into new areas of ministry, it is helpful to be aware of his background.)

Special Interests—What do you enjoy doing on vacations or in your spare time? (This will include hobbies, crafts, sports, and skills as well as other talents which may assist in ministry.)

Expectations—What would you hope to get out of your volunteer ministry? (Most of the time a sensitive pastor can insure that these expectations will be met. Careful placement and appropriate contacts at times throughout the year are key factors in bringing about the fulfillment of expectations.)

Fears—What causes you the greatest feelings of apprehension as you contemplate volunteer ministry? (Frequently, Jeff found, this centered around discipline in the classroom or being "trapped" in the job because no replacements were available. Both of these fears, as well as most others, Jeff understood and was able to assure the volunteer of his full assistance in handling any problems that might arise.)

Preferences—In what capacity and with what age-group would you like to minister? If opportunities are not available, what would be your second choice?

3. Recruitment interviews will include *a written evaluation of spiritual gifts and ministry preferences.* There were several tests that Jeff and his senior pastor found and used at different times. None were perfect but each contributed further insights into helping place each volunteer in the right ministry. Perhaps the most useful was a forced choice test produced by Guidance Assistance Programs (P.O. Box 105, Winfield, IL 60190) simply entitled "Spiritual Gifts." The goal of the test is to help the individual decide how to use his or her spiritual gifts in the church. Actually, it is more a ministry preference questionnaire than a means of definitively identifying spiritual gifts, but Jeff found the test to be an excellent tool for reducing ministry options to those

specifically suited to each volunteer.

4. Recruitment interviews will attempt to *match people to the ministry needs* of the members of the church. This means that if a need exists but the volunteer is not suited to the position or to the team of people with whom he will minister, the person will *not* be placed in that position. The Lord will provide someone else to meet that need.

5. Recruitment interviews will be followed by one to three weeks of *observation by the volunteer*. This requirement gives the new recruit a firsthand picture of the ministry before being placed in a position and allows for a more realistic assessment of what the ministry entails. It also allows potential co-workers to gain firsthand impressions of the volunteer, which assists in making the right placement decision.

6. Recruitment interviews will allow for *feedback from potential co-workers*. "Everybody is smarter than anybody," was a comment Jeff once heard at a Sunday School workshop, and it definitely applies in the recruitment process. Many times fellow volunteer ministers detect strengths or flaws which have been missed in the interview process. Their observations are to be considered a vital part of the interviewing/placement process.

7. The culmination of recruitment interviews will be the *assignment of volunteers to ministry positions*. Jeff found that it was essential for a job description to be given to the volunteer. To make the process more orderly and comfortable for everyone involved, definite starting and concluding dates must be stated.

No process is infallible. Even after going through all of these procedures, there were times when mistakes were made in the assignment of new staff, but never again was there a placement so blatantly inappropriate as that of Marshall Burlington.

There was an unanticipated fringe benefit, however. Those who had gone through the recruitment interview process built meaningful personal relationships with the leadership team and, as a result, demonstrated greater loyalty to the ministry. The net result of this loyalty was that volunteers often continued in their ministry positions longer than previous staff had done, which meant that *less recruitment had to be done*.

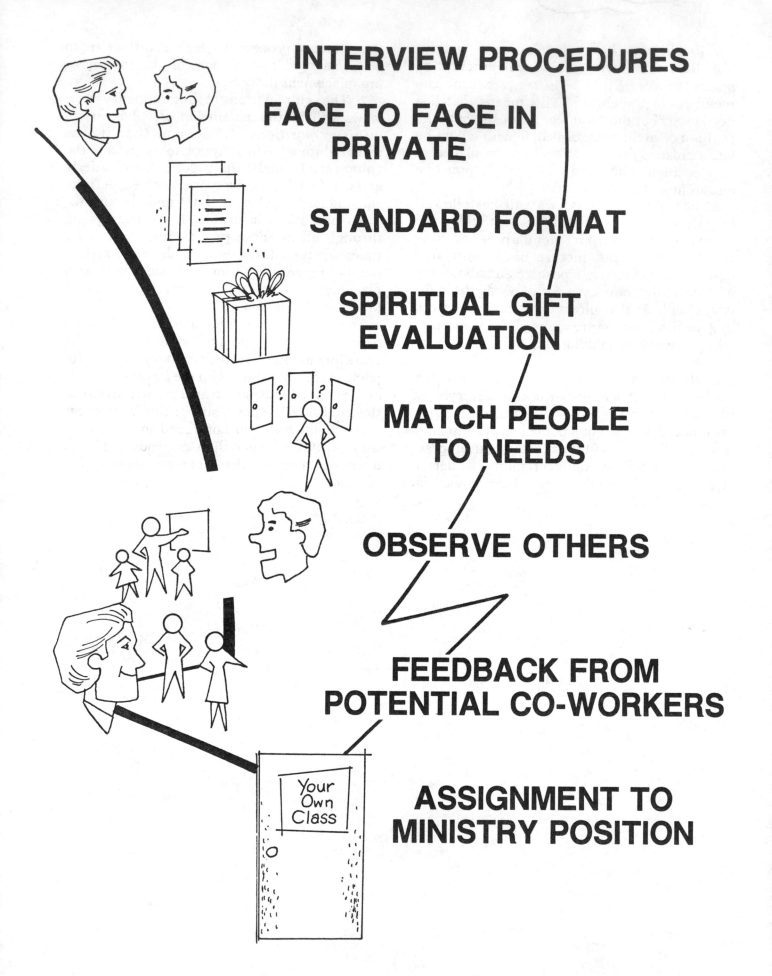

INTERVIEW PROCEDURES

FACE TO FACE IN PRIVATE

STANDARD FORMAT

SPIRITUAL GIFT EVALUATION

MATCH PEOPLE TO NEEDS

OBSERVE OTHERS

FEEDBACK FROM POTENTIAL CO-WORKERS

Your Own Class

ASSIGNMENT TO MINISTRY POSITION

11

Evaluation

At first Jeff rejected the idea.

"It seems so contrary to my ideas about human nature," he told his wife, Rita, at breakfast. "I'm not even sure people will feel comfortable enough to respond positively if they're evaluated on their teaching performance."

"Maybe you need to give people more credit," Rita suggested. "Evaluation is appreciated by teachers who are doing a good job. It's a form of recognition."

As Jeff drove to the church for an evaluation meeting with the middler teaching team, the concept appeared to be a real option. What Rita said made sense. "Perhaps," thought Jeff, "if I'm extremely sensitive about how I approach the process, I can turn evaluation sessions into a recruitment tool—at least a method of retaining an increasing number of quality teachers. That way I might not have to recruit as many new volunteers each year." An interesting possibility.

Nearly a year before at a meeting of the Christian Education Committee, Jeff had raised the idea of evaluating the teaching teams. "I believe if our primary focus is on discovering the strengths of the various teachers and helping them refine and enhance their skills, teacher evaluation could be a productive addition to the program," he had said. After several months of discussion, the committee adopted the plan that he had submitted, and the evaluation process was introduced to the teaching staff at the fall workers conference.

The initial flack had been predictable. "Do you mean to suggest," fired Ford Collins, fourth-grade boys' Sunday School teacher, "that someone, perhaps with no teaching experience, can come into my classroom for a single session and get an accurate picture of how well I'm teaching week-in and week-out?" Sandra Swanson felt especially angered by the process. "After all," she argued, "I've been teaching kindergarten children in this church for 17 years, and if people haven't liked what I've been doing, they would have told me long before now!"

Others expressed similar, though not as defensive, responses at the conference. More concern was expressed to Ernie Larson, chairman of the Christian Education Committee, in the days that followed. But to each person the response was the same: "Pastor Jeff is an easy person to work with. Let's give the process a try, and if it makes your whole team uncomfortable, then we'll reevaluate it—teachers included."

Jeff's role was the key to the idea, and he knew it. He was dealing with volunteers who sincerely wanted to serve the Lord, many of whom felt nervous over having a seminary graduate "peering over their shoulders" in class on Sunday morning. In recognition of their feelings, guidelines were set which, it was hoped, would minimize the teachers' concerns.

1. Teacher teams would be notified two weeks before an evaluation took place in order to allow the teachers to feel they were adequately prepared for the pastor's visit.
2. The evaluation would take place over three consecutive weeks in order to obtain a balanced view of what happens

in the various CE departments.

3. The pastor of Christian education would be in the room from 15 minutes before the scheduled starting time of the class until after the last activity was completed (when the children were turned over to either parents or the church-time leaders).

4. The pastor of Christian education would remain in the department to talk with teachers after each teaching session for as long as the teachers wished to talk. The main discussion, however, would wait until the three weeks were completed.

5. The pastor of Christian education would use an evaluation form with which the teaching team was acquainted in order to reduce the fear of being critiqued in aspects of the teaching art in which the teachers were not trained.

6. The pastor of Christian education would remain as inconspicuous as possible in the room while doing the evaluation.

7. The pastor of Christian education would meet with the teaching teams as a group within two weeks of the in-class evaluation in order to share his observations.

Sandra Swanson's kindergarten was the first teaching team Jeff visited. It was not that he had anything against the kindergarten department. He'd just spent so much time on the phone with Sandra explaining the process and smoothing ruffled feathers that he thought it would be wise to get the process out of the way as quickly as possible. Allowing the evaluation to hang over the veteran teacher's head for months could trigger a buildup of tension and resentment.

The kindergarten evaluation, to Sandra's surprise, was a very positive experience for everyone involved. Though Sandra was not a perfect department leader, she had a number of obvious strengths. Jeff focused on these, suggesting some innovative ways in which these abilities could be channeled to make the teaching experience even more effective. Finally, after nearly an hour and a half of creative affirmation, brainstorming, and instruction, Sandra finally blurted out the question Jeff hoped someone would ask:

"Nobody's perfect, Pastor Jeff!" the veteran admitted. "What did you see that we were doing wrong? Where do we need to improve?"

Jeff was prepared to answer such questions, but he felt reluctant to do so. The meeting had gone so well and so much valuable teacher training had taken place, that he simply didn't want to jeopardize the impact by the negative reaction which even mild criticism could stimulate.

"Come on, Jeff," Sandra chided. "We really want your evaluation on where we could improve."

For the next 20 minutes, Jeff shared helpful observations with the now eager volunteer teachers, offering training resources and practical tips that could strengthen the learning process in the kindergarten department. To his immense relief, it was gracefully received.

Months passed. The third evaluation since the kindergarten teaching team visit had been completed. As Jeff reflected back on the evaluations of the primary and middler departments as well as his time with Sandra Swanson's staff, one fact was obvious: these were dedicated, sincere and, in most cases, gifted people who needed the affirmation, encouragement, and instruction of a person whom they loved and respected. The time and sensitivity he'd invested in the process expanded into a stronger bond of loyalty by teachers toward the church and toward Jeff. There was a new confidence on the part of the teaching staff that they were doing a commendable job in their teaching ministry.

In the years that followed, Jeff's idea of using the evaluation process as a tool for recruiting volunteer workers proved to be valid in two respects. Just as he'd hoped, fewer people had to be recruited because department turnover was lower. Second, Jeff noticed that people who felt affirmed, supported, and assisted at the points of their needs would attract other people to volunteer for teaching. The evaluated people became key influences in the recruitment process.

Despite all the positive aspects of this approach to evaluation, the pastor of Christian education found that the process was simply too time consuming to be practical. After all, it was nearly a luxury to be isolated in one department for an hour and a half, three weeks in a row. Other people needed to see the church's foremost educational resource person during this time. The solution was to train others to do the evaluations.

The next two evaluations gave Jeff the opportunity to teach his age-group coordinators how to assist the teaching teams through the evaluation process. The coordinators were briefed on how to use evaluation as a positive tool, then were given classroom observation assignments.

After each teaching session, Jeff met with the coordinators to discuss the evaluation process. He provided feedback on their comments and observations, the effectiveness of their evaluations, and what should be looked for in the next evaluation session. The response of the coordinators was excellent, for they were upgrading their own skills while building better relationships with their teaching teams and upgrading the quality of the teaching/learning process. It was an "everybody wins" proposition.

In the years that followed, the age-group coordinators remained the primary evaluators of the various departments. But Jeff found himself reentering the process for one of two reasons: to train new age-group coordinators as staff changes occurred and to keep in touch with the grass-roots level of what was happening in the educational ministry of Walnut Heights Bible Church.

TEACHING TEAM EVALUATION FORM

Department_____

Date_____

Evaluator_____

The purpose of this evaluation is to build on the strengths of the teaching team and to expand the horizons of the teachers with regard to the teaching/learning process.

Check evaluated items on the lines (continuums) provided and include comments as frequently as possible.

PERSONAL CHARACTERISTICS OF TEAM MEMBERS
1. Warmth
   Friendly, loving |___|___|___|___| Cold, distant
   Comment:
2. Enthusiasm
   Appropriate |___|___|___|___| Inappropriate
   Comment:
3. Self-revealing
   Open |___|___|___|___| Closed
   Comment:

PREPARATION FOR LEARNING
4. Arrival time of team members
   Early |___|___|___|___| Late
   Comment:
5. Room preparation
   Attractive, uncluttered |___|___|___|___| Dull, messy
   Comment:
6. Lesson preparation
   Mastered |___|___|___|___| Dependent
   Comment:

METHODS EMPLOYED
7. Circle the methods used:

Buzz groups	Discussion	Memorization	Question/answer
Case studies	Drama	Models	Quiz
Cassette tapes	Field trip	Object lessons	Reports
Chalkboard	Filmstrips/slides	Overhead projector	Review
Charts	Flannelgraph	Picture studies	Role play
Conversation	Interview	Playing Bible learning	Singing
Choral readings	Lecture	Problem solving	Skits
Creative writing	Making things	Projects	Story telling
Direct Bible study	Maps	Puppets	Testimony

8. Appropriateness
   Communicated well |___|___|___|___| Unrelated to lesson
   Comment:
9. Skill in use
   Effective |___|___|___|___| Ineffective
   Comment:

TEAMWORK

10. Cooperation among teachers
    Strong |____|____|____|____|____| Weak
    Comment:

11. Discipline
    Appropriate |____|____|____|____|____| Lacking or
    Comment: excessive

12. Organization
    Effective |____|____|____|____|____| Ineffective
    Comment:

CONTENT OF LESSON

13. Biblical basis
    Adequate |____|____|____|____|____| Inadequate
    Comment:

14. Mastery of biblical teachings
    Strong |____|____|____|____|____| Weak
    Comment:

15. Practical application
    Life related |____|____|____|____|____| Theoretical
    Comment:

STUDENT PARTICIPATION

16. During early arrival activities
    Strong |____|____|____|____|____| Weak
    Comment:

17. In large group settings
    Strong |____|____|____|____|____| Weak
    Comment:

18. In small group settings
    Strong |____|____|____|____|____| Weak
    Comment:

IMPACT OF LESSON

19. State simply the apparent lesson
    Aim_____
    _____
    _____

20. To what extent were aims accomplished?
    Largely accomplished |____|____|____|____| Largely
    Comment: unaccomplished

21. Evidence of learning
    Strong |____|____|____|____|____| Weak
    Comment:

SUMMARY

22. What were the strengths of the teaching/learning process observed today?
    _____
    _____
    _____
    _____

23. What were the weaknesses of the teaching/learning process observed today?
    _____
    _____
    _____

24. What strength can be used even more effectively? How?
    _____
    _____
    _____
    _____

12

Recruitment as Shepherding

It must have been a dream. Jeff couldn't remember. It seemed so real, so vivid, so comfortable. . . .

As far as his eye could see, shepherds moved like ants among the gently rolling hills. Westerly breezes whispered among the patches of trees which seemed to frame the pastures, creating a gigantic patchwork quilt in shades of green across the luscious hills. Yet, oddly enough, something was missing. There were no sheep. Just shepherds, talking and waiting. But waiting for what?

Trudging into the pastures himself, he wandered the rolling hills. Jeff was amazed at the diversity he found among the people present. Primitive tribesmen from the "outback" of Australia, Scotsmen with their kilts and sheep dogs, family farmers from neatly run farms in Ohio, Palestinian nomads from the Negev, rugged herdsmen from the seemingly endless land grant acreage in Texas. Their languages and dress were as diverse as the lands from which they'd come and yet, to his further amazement, conversations flowed like the gentle murmur of Appalachian streams.

From group to group Jeff wandered, listening, watching, tempted to question the uniformly hospitable strangers about the purpose of their gathering and the object of their waiting. Yet each time the words were formed on his lips he could not break into the conversation with the people.

Common interests dominated the friendly chatter. Favorite breeds of sheep constantly entered the discussions: Romeldale, Shropshire, Panama, Corriedale, Romney, and other equally unfamiliar names emerged as breeds were described and lovingly compared.

Unfamiliar? Yes, and yet not strange and unknown. The more he listened to the conversations, the more Jeff realized he knew (or was coming to know, as sometimes happens in dreams) about the sheep being discussed.

Problems of breeding, feeding, health care, protection, shearing, and a thousand other details crowded conversation after conversation. Marketing of products occasionally surfaced in discussions, but only briefly as the shepherds appeared most interested in their flocks and in the personal needs of individual sheep.

Once again Jeff was tempted to inquire about the purpose of the gathering when the myriad conversations suddenly melted away into silence. Heads turned as if on an inaudible command, and each eye became riveted on a Shepherd who stood quietly on a grassy knoll. Yet he appeared to belong to each group, each language, each type of native dress.

A hush of anticipation settled over the multitude. The waiting was over. Whatever had been anticipated was about to happen.

There was no fanfare as the Shepherd began to walk down the knoll toward a group of shepherds. Quickly, He blended into the crowd, while at the same time (and this is one of the ways in which Jeff knew that the events were a dream of some sort) the Shepherd remained perfectly visible to everyone present. No fanfare was needed, for His very presence commanded the total respect of every living being.

Now He was in the thick of a crowd on the flatland between a stand of birch trees and the steep incline which led to the ridge on the west. He had paused beside a shepherd whose gaze had fallen, as if in genuine embarrassment, to the feet of the One to whom everyone else looked in anticipation.

"Joshua," said the Shepherd in a voice that barely exceeded a whisper and yet was totally audible wherever the sheep-loving people stood.

"Joshua," He spoke again with a greater strength that commanded the sheepish herdsman to look Him in the eye. "I will present to you a reward that will never tarnish or fade away. Here are the people whom you shepherded during your lifetime."

With that, all of the angry people on whom the simple shepherd had poured the oil of healing, all the growing people to whom he had fed words of encouragement, all of the confused people to whom he had provided insight and direction, all of the lonely people to whom he was available, all of the healthy people to whom he was a model, as well as ones who needed the correction, rebuke, punishment, or instruction which he had provided—all came and formed an appreciative crowd around the embarrassed herdsman. One by one the people expressed in warm measure the deep-felt appreciation which each had experienced in a lifetime of following their shepherd.

Ages seemed to have passed (as could only happen in a dream) and still the people came and spoke. Sometimes tears glistened in their eyes. Then they drifted back into their own circle of friends. Finally, just as it appeared that the line of friends might come to an end, there came a second gathering of sheep—new people. These, though seemingly not familiar with the modest shepherd, had been touched by the lives of the people to whom the shepherd had ministered directly. Each person told of how he had been cared for in ways learned from Joshua. This group was far larger than the first crowd because for every person to express appreciation in the first group there were 5, 10, 25, or even 100 who stood in line to add their appreciation to the unassuming tender of this flock.

About the time that this second flow of people had dwindled to a trickle, another flock of sheep gathered around, then a fourth and a fifth, as if the ever enlarging crowds of people

appreciative for the faithful service of one conscientious shepherd would never fade away or cease.

All the time that Jeff was observing the events taking place around this first shepherd, the great Shepherd had remained active. He had moved from shepherd to shepherd initiating the same chain of events for herdsmen as far as the eye could see. Endless lines of appreciative people formed a fluid pattern of shepherds both expressing and receiving affirmation for obedient service to the master Shepherd.

Gradually, the picture blurred, much the way binoculars do when trying to refocus from some distant scene to an object close at hand. Sounds too became indistinguishable, a gentle murmur of contented voices. Perhaps the dream was over—or could this be what the Prophet Joel might have referred to as a vision?

Either way, the pastor of Christian education still had to finish his preparation for the Christian education staff meeting the following evening. His Bible lay open to 1 Peter 5:1-4. That's what he was! That's what they were! Shepherds—shepherding the flocks of God.

For a few moments Jeff thought back over his ministry at Walnut Heights Bible Church. Maybe that was why recruiting and training of staff for the education program seemed so much less difficult in recent days. He had not simply been recruiting workers. He had been shepherding one of God's flocks.

His thoughts wandered from person to person—old and young, male and female, sophisticated and naive, all with one common bond: Jeff had touched each one in a time of need.

There was Andy, the fifth-grade teacher in Sunday School who had lost his job due to personnel cutbacks in middle management. Jeff was no career counselor, but he was available to listen, question, provide feedback, pray, suggest resource people within the church and community, and finally rejoice when Andy landed a new job.

Larry and Charlene also came to mind. Charlene was a self-assured professional woman in her mid-20s when she began teaching in the early childhood children's church program at the church. Jeff's first impressions had been verified throughout her first year of teaching. She was capable, sensitive, organized, and loved by her little learners. Then shortly into her second year of children's church leadership, "Miss Composure" appeared to be falling apart.

A phone call by the pastor of Christian education served to bring the "Larry" problem to light. Charlene just couldn't decide whether she loved him enough to take the chance of losing her career in favor of a life of "wifery," as she perceived it.

Shepherding had taken the form of counseling this time—to each individually, then both together. The decision was not an easy one. Though Larry and Charlene were able to work through certain apprehensions each had about self-worth and the institution of marriage, their final conclusion was not to marry.

Other shepherding events flooded Jeff's mind. There was the hospitalized department leader he'd spent time with, whose doctor suspected cancer. A single mother needed a sounding board when her ex-husband failed to send Christmas gifts to the children, leaving her stuck with the question, "Doesn't Daddy love *us*, either?" The club leader who knew that Jeff was interested in him and could share "very special" prayer requests with him, both as friend and pastor. Memories of shepherded people marched through his mind accompanied by the feelings of celebration associated with an Independence Day parade.

Gradually, the dawn had come.

Jeff had come to realize that recruitment and shepherding are inseparably linked together. Without the balm of shepherding, recruiting would be almost unbearable. Without the practical consequences of recruiting, shepherding would become inbred, isolated, abstract. On the other hand, with shepherding, recruiting became an exciting opportunity to extend present ministries; and with recruiting, shepherding became a natural expression of God's love toward others.

Jeff's mandate was becoming increasingly clear. Tomorrow evening's talk to the Christian education staff would take the form of a shepherd talking to his under-shepherds. Thoughts, experiences, and biblical insights would be shared in order to encourage and lift the entire staff, to inspire and permeate them with loving shepherding principles.

The message that Tuesday night was quite simple. It was built around the sign posted at railroad crossings: **STOP! LOOK! LISTEN!**

Stop to think about the people with whom you are ministering
... their joys ... their hurts ... their pressures ... their successes.

Stop to pray for the people with whom you are ministering
... responding to their stated needs ... their nonverbal clues ... their observable frustrations.

Stop to switch from task orientation to a personal perspective
... not so much program as people ... not so much numbers as needs ... not so much doing as being.

Look at people's faces to become aware of their sensitivity
... at their smiles to perceive their receptivity ... at their eyes to share their celebration of life ... at their shoulders to understand the loads they carry.

Look at people from their own perspective
... what is shaping them? ... what is concerning them? ... what is crowding them? ... what is pleasing them?

Look for God in people
... through His Word ... through the predictable crises of life ... through responses to the mistakes of others.

Listen to what is being said
... when it is not convenient ... when it is uncomfortable ... when it is obviously biased ... when someone less wise is speaking.

Listen to what is felt
... when words mislead ... when smiles obscure ... when eyes cry out ... when confusion reigns.

Listen to what God says
... through the Bible ... through God's Spirit ... through circumstances ... through people ... through rejection ... through life.

Though the words, the approach, the context of Pastor Jeff's message were fresh to his audience, the ministry staff of Walnut Heights Bible Church recognized something very familiar about it. A few of them smiled to themselves. It was a theme they had seen emerge, grow, and blossom in their pastor of Christian education over the years. He was living it.